M000048267

Peter Swinnen
Nikolaus Hirsch

A.J. LODE JANSSENS

1.47 mbar

SPECTOR BOOKS
CIVA

FOR A GENTLE PRESSURE	Peter Swinnen	6
MODEL LIFE – THINKING THROUGH BUILDINGS	Nikolaus Hirsch	10
SYMBIOSIS & SYMBICLE: A RETROSPECTIVE	A.J. Lode Janssens	18
A BALLOON HOME (EXHIBITION)	Filip Dujardin	33
A TEMPORARY DATUM (EXHIBITION VIEWS)	Peter Swinnen & A.J. Lode Janssens	48
THE END OF THE FUTURE	Bart Decroos	69
UNRAVELED ARCHIVE		81
THE HANDKERCHIEF PRINCIPLE	Guy Mouton	144
EDUCATION BETWEEN THOUGHT AND ACTION	Elke Couchez	150
LIVING AND BUILDING WITH AIR	Pieter Uyttenhove	159
1979	Herman Selleslags	171
BIOGRAPHIES		187

A.J. Lode Janssens, 1974

FOR A GENTLE PRESSURE

Peter Swinnen

It's extremely difficult to get a hold of A.J. Lode Janssens, both literally and figuratively. For the past two decades the Belgian architect and educator has been living in voluntary exile, resisting all forms of public life. There are many reasons why to not publish on Janssens and his spatial work, the foremost reason being that he himself has always actively resisted any form of "publicity"—a trait that can be traced back to his heartfelt love-hate relationship with the architecture discipline. Janssens has always been enthralled by architecture's experimental possibilities while being equally appalled by its presumptuous and often superficial nature. It's as if he's constantly on the lookout to settle an account in and with architecture. So why not grant Janssens the anonymity and serenity he so aspires to have?

Sometimes architecture is so authentic and brutally honest that it simply cannot remain concealed. During the thirty years of his architectural practice, Janssens produced over a hundred projects and many critical research trajectories, with a portfolio ranging from private dwellings to public-school complexes. This broad yet consistent oeuvre is however not the subject of this volume. There is one project—a highly personal and experimental one—that stands out above all the others: the temporary dome dwelling he built for his family. The headstrong, syncretic project enabled Janssens to transcend all conventions of and normative claims on architecture's technical performance and juridical statute, imposed by technical and administrative authorities. Architecture *hors catégorie*.

For his unsolicited experiment Janssens decided to become the client himself—or, more accurately, the lab rat. His client-driven projects made him feel uncomfortable when it came to maximizing the experimental potential of his proposals. Hence, between 1973 and 1982, the architect embarked on an obsessive architectural trip, living in and with nature, using but an ultrathin PVC foil and some tent fragments. To minimize the difference between inside and outside, the air-supported dome employed an extremely light top pressure, of but 1.47 mbar on average. Just enough to keep the structure raised.

The temporary dome exercise is clearly a child of its time, architecturally and sociopolitically. Though Janssens has always insisted that it could not be reduced to an ecological, technological, or formal exercise: it was foremost about phenomenologically testing life itself.

Clearly, its de-architecturalized structure, with its polyurethane-coated satellites, can be linked to other inflatable devotees like Archigram, Ant Farm, François Dallegret, Coop Himmelb(l)au, and Haus-Rucker-Co, among others. Though a central difference set Janssens' dome apart: it was not an exhibit, but a 1:1 model meant for actual living—live tested over a ten-year period. In total, Janssens and his family would experience 4,000 of earth's revolutions under their skin-like ceiling, equaling 146 lunar months, or better still: ten solar orbits. A more than intimate cohabitation with nature and the cosmos.

The Balloon, sun rising, 1975

The present volume is the first post-factum commons on the project, which Janssens himself had in mind when starting his self-built experiment. His original goal was to share the insights of his research-by-design only after the experiment had ended. This, however, never happened. Janssens considers himself, above all, an architectural educator, conducting pedagogy through trial and error and unique live experiments. The Balloon (including its final collapse in 1982) allowed him to educate in a hands-on manner—himself and his family being the primary students. Later, as head of the architecture department of the Sint-Lucas School of Architecture (in Brussels and Ghent) and in his engagements within the ILAUD network, alongside Giancarlo De Carlo and Peter Smithson, his undeterred attitude would manifest further. And that is perhaps the most generous and upright "lesson" A.J. Lode Janssens brought to the architectural table: experiment more!

Briefly awakening this gentle giant seems more than urgent. His unsolicited and sensual thinking can serve a future society in unforeseen ways. Beyond the dichotomic fallacy of success and failure, it is a unique story about a socially engaged architect capable of walking between raindrops, whatever the odds. An intriguing rarity.

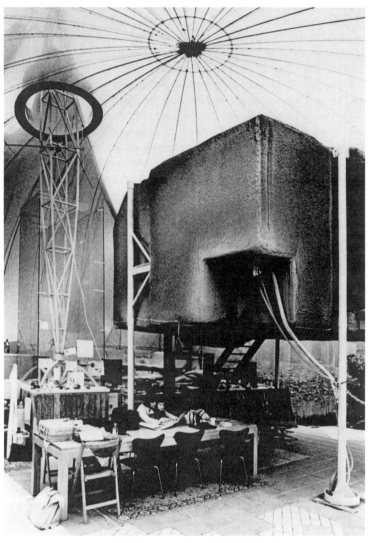

The Balloon, parents' moon lander, 1975

MODEL LIFE – THINKING THROUGH BUILDINGS

Nikolaus Hirsch

A photograph from 1971 shows a man, an architect, working under a clear plastic tarp. It is A.J. Lode Janssens, thirty years old, building a model of his Balloon. A promise of liberation caught from within.

Can an architect inhabit a model, both as a practitioner who conceptualizes space and someone who literally lives in it? How does Janssens deal with a double problem of representation—how "real" the model is, whether it represents something else than itself, and the question of himself, the architect, as a figure of representation?

Making Models

Models embody something that is not yet there, or that would otherwise remain abstract. This probably explains why architectural metaphors are so intriguing for philosophical discourse, as the cipher for designing worlds. From Plato's Cave to G. W. F. Hegel's pyramid; the Tower of Babel to Friedrich Nietzsche's metaphors of fortress, columbarium, honeycomb, and spiderweb; Gilles Deleuze's fold to Peter Sloterdijk's sphere to various conceptions of the cloud and the platform, philosophical concepts became architectures and political states became buildings.

Similar conceptual models can be seen in architectural theory. In his *Essay on Architecture* from 1753, Jesuit priest and architectural theorist Marc-Antoine Laugier reconstructed the primitive hut as an explanatory model of the discipline and of the beginning of human habitat. A few decades later, Quatremère de Quincy added the tent and the cave, and in the mid-nineteenth century, Gottfried Semper defined the cloth as the origin of all architecture.

Yet practicing architects traditionally use models in a far more pragmatic way: they describe a time that is yet to come. They manifest a project; projections toward the future. Foresight is what distinguishes architecture from the spontaneous making of concrete things. Since its beginnings, the discipline has had to live with a schizophrenic condition, a conceptual split between its etymological components: *arche* (the beginning or first principle) and *techne* (craft). The best architectural models convey this ambivalent status, oscillating between process and form, between conceptualization and

A.J. Lode Janssens building a 1:10 model of the Balloon, 1971

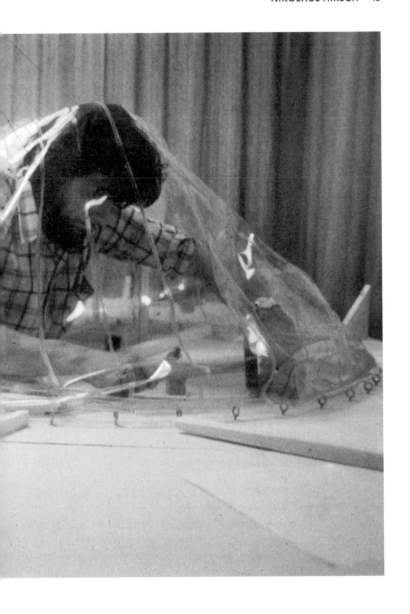

contextualization. They eventually gain a status of their own and become vectors of experimentation.

A.J. Lode Janssens' project is such an experiment. It is "real," yet it is a model. It is built on a real plot, with real material, housing real people. But it continues to be a model—a model for a different life—from the outset defined by Janssens as a temporary project, with a permit for a ten-year experiment and an eventual exit strategy.

Life and Work

When Janssens built his own home he implicitly or explicitly questioned the modernist concept of the house as a realm separated from the world of production. In fact, he strictly avoided the term "house," as if it was a contaminated typology. And it is—the house is an ideological construct, dating back to the beginnings of modernism, wherein the dichotomy between the house as the sphere of reproduction and the factory as the site of production is fundamental.

Janssens' project questions this separation and can be read as an emblem of a dissolution: his model is a structure that transcends the boundaries between domestic spaces and spaces of work. And this dissolution increasingly became a normality in the early twenty-first century. New forms of production imply the enmeshing of work and life to the point that they become indistinguishable. This condition clashes with the very purpose of the domestic interior, which, since its invention, was supposed to exist in opposition to the sphere of work. It is at odds with what Walter Benjamin described as the essence of the bourgeois interior: "For the private individual, the place of dwelling is for the first time opposed to the place of work. The former constitutes itself as interior. Its complement is the office. The private individual, who in the office has to deal with reality, needs the domestic interior to sustain him in his illusions."[1] Janssens' Balloon is emancipated from the bourgeois interior. It is both inside and outside, protected and exposed. In this new domestic environment everything is integrated into an expanded architectural practice: living room, kitchen, beds. It was like—in Janssens' words—"experimenting with life. An empirical residence. Housing oneself temporarily. Work-in-progress."[2]

To Janssens' discomfort, his experimental life became a spectacle. Thousands of uninvited visitors wanted to see this live experiment—the escape became a *site*, reinforcing the inescapability of commodification. In the age of "immaterial labor," the domestic sphere is neither a counter-space nor an appendix of the workplace but its epicenter. The result is biopolitical fusion of life and work, with all its utopian and dystopian potentials.

Spaceship Home

The Balloon's primary material is air. What sounds simple and basic is (and has been, since the beginnings of the ecological debate) a contested element. You cannot take air for granted. According to Peter Sloterdijk, air has lost its innocence. He describes a metaphysical history of enclosed spaces, utopian or pragmatic pods and domes, real and fantastical atmospheres or ecosystems. Modernity, Sloterdijk argues, has long been a matter of a double agenda of control and liberation through a sort of air conditioning. And we live now, of course, with the constant knowledge that we have stressed the system beyond repair.

This extreme conditioning in turn has created a new era: the Anthropocene, a human-made planetary reality. This, almost ironically, burdens humanity with an unprecedented responsibility with respect to its own survival other lifeforms as well.

Even before humankind first saw a photograph of the whole Earth and the Club of Rome met to write about the limits of growth, we have long known that infinite expansion is impossible. Yet the critique of growth has fueled powerful reactions that have taken place both in and to our built environments, from deregulation and degradation to speculation, derivation, and exclusion. Architects and engineers, toiling daily at the coalface of economic expansion, are complicit in the perpetuation of growth. They are also in a unique position to contribute to its disavowal.

The work of practitioners like the Metabolists, Buckminster Fuller, Frei Otto, Ant Farm and, in the Belgian context, A.J. Lode Janssens, have been seismographs of that crisis. While Fuller exposed the vulnerability of "spaceship earth" with his geodesic domes, Janssens' Balloon focused on the small scale of a spaceship dwelling. A comment on suburbia, on the house, on the family.

After World War II, Belgium went through a process of massive suburbanization. The single-family house became the dominant building type, built in residential subdivisions, ribbon developments, or as piecemeal developments scattered through the landscape, without any further environmental considerations. The Balloon's neighborhood was such a generic suburbia.

Protection is the primary function of the sphere. The house fundamentally concerns the question of insulation. Spheres, as described by Sloterdijk, function like a membrane or a sensitive wall that acts as an immune system by preventing undesirable things from entering, yet claiming to provide a liberated life. Security and freedom.

A.J. Lode Janssens' Balloon presents an unsolvable tension: it is both a home to inhabit and model for a different life—or, in other words, the contradictory condition of an inhabitable model. Yet, its categorical problem might be the project's greatest potential: the architectural model as a medium in which political metaphors and physical manifestations collapse into one phenomenon, as a construction that is not quite a "house," a term that Janssens wholly rejected.

[1]   Walter Benjamin, "Paris, the Capital of the Nineteenth Century," in *The Arcades Project*, trans. Howard Eiland and Kevin McLaughlin (Cambridge, MA: Harvard University Press, 2002), 8.
[2]   A.J. Lode Janssens in "A Temporary Datum," page 50.

1:10 model of the Balloon, 1971

SYMBIOSIS & SYMBICLE: A RETROSPECTIVE

A.J. Lode Janssens

1969 / 1973–1982 / 1986
design   experiment   self-build home

We are still surviving modernism (B. Hoesli)
    Ceçi n'est pas de l'architecture, ce sont des styles (Le Corbusier)
    A big step for mankind (N. Armstrong)
        Nothing is impossible (P. Cook)
            Imagine… (J. Lennon)
            Une machine à habiter (Le Corbusier)
            Menschsein heißt, Utopie haben (P. Tillich)
    Utopia functions in design like the hypothesis does in science
        Architecture does not need to be permanent
        Architecture does not need to be
We are in search of sheltering life
        Which life
            Which shelter
            Which approach

Zeitgeist
Whenever I started to design, I always reflected upon **the current zeit-geist** and the **common worldview** and how architecture could act in a meaningful way within this context. The zeitgeist exists and we are part of it. You can alienate yourself from it, or you can try to understand it and take a position. The phenomena of both zeitgeist and common worldviews truly fascinate me. Hence, how I could understand these and how then this critical understanding could or should inspire the architecture I was about to design were recurring driving forces throughout my career as architectural and urban designer.

At the time that the Symbiosis & Symbicle project—the Balloon—was developed, we were part of the zeitgeist of the 1960s and 1970s, with its very specific characteristics. I experienced the movement of May '68 as a reaction to the centralization of power; domination over people; capitalism, clientelism, etc. At the same time, I felt how it promoted emancipation, participation, pluralism, redistribution, and ethical recovery. People responded to the **alienation of the individual** in society, but from my point of view, the purpose of the movement was to renew participation in a common "good," as opposed to personal profit. In light of this, **participation** became a crystallizing concept in my work.

I would describe the content of that revolution, as I experienced it, as a liberalizing, emancipating movement that pushed forward all levels and aspects of society (expanding social consciousness, breaking open power structures, redefining societal goals). It felt like a much-needed reaction against the erosion of values and of the "love" or longing for wisdom (also called philo-sophy), of the structure of society and equality, of healthcare and culture, of meaningful places and historical awareness, of identity and true participation that had been going on far too long time and that increasingly threatened a real, "human" quality in our way of life.

The crisis and the new knowledge and concepts it forged on many different levels of society also evoked the dream that in turn inspired me to think of other architectural concepts. For example, space travel and its spin-offs left a deep impression on me (a renewed cosmic awareness). Changes in living patterns and societal patterns led to a new agenda, marked by idealism (utopia), social programs, and technological ambitions. Thus, for example, housing became communal housing, alternative living, self-building, etc.

As an architect, I belonged to the modernist movement. With **modernity**, a fundamental inquiry begins, and man places himself at the center of the cosmos, which he wants to put at his service and dominate (the transition from realism to idealism to **ideology**). The concept of progress and the idea of make-ability become important cornerstones. Increasingly, mankind creates its own reality. In the world of architecture, methodology and technology dominate ideas about form (Christopher Alexander, Archigram and Peter Cook, Cedric Price …), and the same applies to the sophisticated architecture philosophies of Kenzō Tange and Kiyonori Kikutake's metabolism. Concurrently, much effort goes into developing new auxiliary methods for the design process (Alexander's pattern language, Stichting Architecten Research-application, structure and process planning). Architecture without architects and architecture on paper become new models.

In contrast to today, I felt that the architectural culture that I was educated in lagged behind the times dramatically. Already during my education I felt short-sheeted and experienced what was offered as vocational training rather than as an initiation into a general discipline. I expressed this most acutely in the manifesto I wrote in 1963 (in my fourth year of architecture studies). I observed how architecture was balanced between the art of building and simply constructing (like romantic neo-farmsteads and allotment villas). And how it eagerly offered itself up to construction-industry schemes and the culture of contractors. Besides research into materials by engineers, little or no relevant research in architectural design and conceptualization was done. **I experienced architecture as being self-centered** and increasingly perceived as a status symbol. This visibly manifested on the one hand in "style" concepts, and on the other hand in protectionist heritage management. In other words: narcissism and the continuous reinterpretation of its own (internal) vocabulary (jargon). Architecture in this sense was never professionally attractive to me. I was always busy with minimizing, rejecting, and selecting commissions, although I had to ensure that I could still provide a living for myself and my family.

This profound discontent with the architecture world manifested itself quite strongly when, at the end of the 1960s, we started thinking about building our own home. At first, I made a few designs based on the functionalist-modernist approach common at the time, which I had gained experience in through my practice. But how could that be an answer to the zeitgeist? How could that generate alternative ways of living fit for a changing worldview and contribute to a utopian way of thinking? My education had been almost exclusively focused on the sedentary, perfectly in line with the "my home, my castle" credo that promoted a domestic culture I had come to despise—one driven by ownership and (cultural) stagnation. It was clear to me that the architecture that emerged from this domestic culture reduced life to programmed patterns (related to status, style, and habit). I was (and am) convinced that the tendency toward permanent settlement is unnatural and the way in which this translates into permanent, almost unremovable architectural is often also permanently damaging our living environment. So, the question then became: what could be a home of a more ephemeral quality, breaking away from the ruling domestic culture, real estate dictates, and (old) construction-industry schemes.

Principles for Designing from within the zeitgeist
To me, designing has to be about supporting (ever evolving) life and not about romanticized dwelling (and even less about the architect's house). Hence, it must not be concerned with an architectural work in first place, but rather, and more importantly, with an **attitude**, a way of life. From this "baseline," I formulated some principles that I considered to be fundamental to develop another architectural culture, one that would be more sensitive to our living environment (both societal and natural).

Life is a cosmic happening that places mental (living) space above physical space, which is circumstantial and time and place dependent. Man does not live in a house or building; he lives in the cosmos (the mental space). **As humans, we are predestined to live in space.** Personal space is merely accommodation that responds to the restrictions inherent to being human, not inherent to our "mission." The mental space (without scale, an immaterial part of community and cosmos) is not an illusion; on the contrary, it is more real (existential) than physical private space. We need to liberate ourselves from the hermeticism of contemporary (architectural) spatial perception, and its artificial value (aesthetics, culture) needs to be demystified.

The mission for humans is to shape and give meaning to a place. The place is temporary (where one casts anchor)—it cannot be property—it can never be an eternal occupation of "sacred" ground. The perspective remains nomadic: the finding (again and again) of that place (along the way). Being underway is actually an act of continuous creation. Man does not need a definitive anchoring; he does, however, need to cast an anchor, a sense of space and time, and a point of reference (a home halfway = a point along the way for farewells and reunions). A shelter as a true transitory home.

I have always had an overpowering awareness of **life as an ultimate phenomenon of creation** and **symbiosis as a metabolic condition of existence**. Past (= learning)—Present (= being, thinking and doing)—Future

(= aspiring). Holding on to life is paradoxically only possible by sur-viving (to live on). Living on is only possible through the preservation of nature and through our capacity to live together. Being is **dasein** (Heidegger), as in the deep awareness of being somewhere, situated. This *dasein* includes a living form of living together. **To belong!** *Dasein* distinguishes between **a native perception of space (womb)** and **an empirical experience of space.**

The existential dilemma.
Existing means being outside of oneself (ex-), focused on other people and on the "outside." Man is simultaneously an individual and a social being, subject to laws of conflicting interests inherent to his existence. He is part of nature/society, yet everything he creates is intrinsically culture. Nature/society is both beneficent and violent. All of existence, thus, continually takes place between opposite poles. The secret hides in how these poles are always simultaneously present, which creates a constant tension that humans have to accept/get accustomed to as a source of life: **symbiosis.**

The metabolic process.
Life (human and natural) is a constant shapeshifting and mutational process (metabolism).
Humans living together is based on the paradoxical aspiration to form cells, to be united. This extreme unification actually means creating new life, which in turn entails splitting off.
Splitting off, however, in order to reunite: **symbiosis.**

The nomadic essence.
Mankind possesses an inborn and natural mobility, which is enhanced by his surroundings (impulse of space, the cosmos). He was originally nomadic, but has become an ardent tourist (perversion).
Restricting this intrinsic mobility is unnatural; "settlement" ensues. Living becomes inhabiting, becomes housing, becomes static, becomes stone… being underway then becomes a petrified life, trapped… There is an urgent need for a new (self-renewing) nomadism, between underway and home as **symbiosis.**

Philosophy behind the Project
What preoccupied me as architect was projecting, experimenting (searching), and philosophizing (or rather, longing for wisdom), and passing this

on (via my pedagogical practice). That was my real mode of living, what kept me busy: **the reliving of utopian thinking, the appreciation of the experiment, the embodiment of the research, and a thoroughly developed theoretical framework (understanding the purpose) to found these all on. Besides a fascination for technology, I also had a clear concern for ecology and integration with nature.**

The wealth of inspiring innovative trends (1945–75) was so extraordinarily large that participating in research, the experiment, the innovation, was a must for me. The mission that I finally gave myself was not to build a house (nor the architectural concerns and domestic culture usually associated with it), but the execution of an experiment, a trial-and-error investigation.

An experiment contains a preliminary study (research), a program and a time span. Thus, the assignment became: **spend ten years thinking about and working on a conscious way of life and the physical conditions that are needed to make it possible and to accompany it**. Hence, the mission became to create a conditional environment within a softly supported piece of nature that could offer maximum developmental freedom as well as the necessary metabolic support for the life of a family.

An approach that was **syncretic**; not (only) following reason, but also consciously deploying the symbiotic coupling of thinking and doing. The thinking (longing for wisdom) requires the doing (entrepreneurial), and the doing (trial and error) corrects and stimulates the thinking (investigation).

Methodically, the experiment is an **activity on the scale of 1:1** and therefore it has a more comprehensible participatory capacity (for the family). There was a striving toward **a form of de-architecturalization**: an attempt to not make architecture, but also to not slip into anti-architecture. The main attempt was to make sense, to create (new) meaning through the design of a particular experimental project.

The philosophy behind the project developed as radiation of the zeitgeist contained the following aspects:
- Reparation of the symbiotic balance between "settling" and "always being underway."

The central dome as shelter (transitory home) became the point of reference to which we could return at any time and which was also conceived as a possible temporary accommodation for friends—when, for example, we would be nomads again. Due to its radical nature, this standpoint brings up the question of whether it is responsible (and to which extent) to bring children into such an unstable adventure (even though every life, of course, is intrinsically unstable). For us, this became **a latent issue** that dominated the majority of the design sessions.

- Revaluing the human/nature relationship.
  To be able to be open to living with, in and according to nature (and equally with, in, and according to society) and to co-create meaning in this relationship, it was physically necessary to have a protective possibility for retreat, and a psychological return to one's self for reflection. For this reason, besides making the collective living spaces as open as possible, the individual cells were as closed as possible.

- Intensification of the community structure.
  I propagated from within my professional practice the communal living concept, and I coached many groups using that concept. I also constantly strived for group practices. We lived together intensely with our neighbors. Never was there any case of territorial boundaries whatsoever. Both sites formed one big "wild" and free nature area to the great joy of the kids of both families. The siblings and grandparents of both households became like family to each other.
  We were highly engaged in kindergarten and elementary education at the Kakelbont School. Together with a group of progressive parents and teachers, we visited Steiner schools, Jenaplan schools, and Montessori schools in Belgium and the Netherlands to learn from each other. We did all of this to support the social integration of our children.

In forming the concept, the contagious enthusiasm of gardener Louis Le Roy with his principle of "soft guidance" of nature led to a breakthrough: we would go and **live in and with nature**: not the building but the natural world became primordial. Thus, the project became a transparent membrane that was not a mirror (for domestic culture) on the inside, because the "external" (society and nature) remained the mirror, and from the outside it did not display a facade (status symbol), because the inside (the soul) would remain entirely observable; a veritable **second skin after the model of the physiognomy of humankind**. The human skin, after all, although it is not transparent, is reliably telling, and in permanent metabolism; physiognomy is form and expression in accordance with inner values, with the soul and character. The main features are its layering and permanent mutation. This is what a dignified human architecture should aspire to.

The Design

In the end, the design concept became a rather strict translation of the proposed principles. I once formulated it like this: "Co-living with nature does not support building from petrified life, which parasitizes on the 'sacred' land. The building is merely a transparent membrane, a millimeter boundary, in order for nature, and not the walls, to limit our living space. There are no walls with windows, dressed with wallpaper and paintings; there are no ceilings with mounted chandeliers… no domestic culture. There is only the soil, the earth to which all life orients itself. The conditioned (enclosed) bit of nature in the interior space largely remains 'nature,' and the floor has the character of garden tiles and terraces. It is a 'living' building in the most literal sense: it is not static, it moves constantly, shrinking and swelling, breathing. It is organic, it has a skin, muscles and nerves, and a heart upon which its existence depends. It is not durable and not finished. It is constantly undergoing metabolic and shapeshifting processes inside and outside, under the influence of nature and ourselves."

In giving form to the concept, several intense experiences served as inspiration. The preliminary studies and the conceptual design included a "kids' home" as a kind of dock for units and a carport area (with a connectable Symbicle), both as annexes to the central living area. As a whole, it was intentionally not based on a functional layout (living, cooking, sleeping, bathing) but on a foundational psychological principle: the whole was as open as possible to stimulate general community building (family), but the units as a counterbalance were as closed as possible to the individual.

The central dome (the membrane) was inspired by the "origin," the womb as existential temporary shelter (family building and the birth of a third child dominated our life at the time). The dome (not a balloon, as it later became

Balloon model, scale 1/50, 1971

called) was anchored in the place where the family landed with a (moveable) unit, the "lunar module" (the 1969 moon landing was imprinted on my memory). Initially, every child was provided with a small tent in the central space, but this idea quickly turned out to be too simplistic (not feasible in daily life). Children are initially dependent, but steadily grow toward independence.

We designed a dock (the "umbilical cord") as a symbol of an element "pointing out" toward the wide world, that at the same time fulfilled a function of welcoming and receiving. The independent children's units were originally meant as caravans that would dock, with which they could later fly out of when they gained their independence. This idea was also abandoned and replaced by units that were inspired by the parents' units. Their units were gathered together in a large collective tent (also known as the "kids' area") that was connected to the central dome.

The mobile cell, the Symbicle, would provide for the needs of the family (five people) for a temporary stay anywhere between one day and six months at another location (with any longer period of stay, renting locally was considered more logical). When at home, the mobile cell would be parked under the tarp of the carport and (flexibly) coupled to the residential dome, extendable for specific purposes (e.g., a guest room). The mobile unit would be built on an existing chassis (we were thinking of a Citroën H Van) with fixed utilities. Building upon that, a translucent pneumatic dome area would provide the necessary living and working space. This design solution was finally abandoned not only due to high costs, but also because it would probably exceed my technical capacities. Plus, the caravan we had purchased at the beginning of 1973 amply fulfilled all of these functions: from holiday home ("always on the road") to bedroom for the momentarily incomplete experiment; from design desk on the property of a new client to a work shed for experiment; from kids' playhouse to guest house. Hence, it fulfilled the program of the Symbicle.

During the **realization of the project**, it became clear that town planning, administrative, and legal apparatuses were not suited for experimental building, which meant that much energy was wasted and abnormal risks were taken. A planning permission was granted solely **on the basis of experimental value and only for ten years** (unlike a normal planning permission). Loans and insurances were problematic.

Design = Sensemaking

The experimental approach was based on the principle of: **designing is (ought to be) resigning.** Every social and physical "grounding" of architecture first demands a critical and plural reflection. Architecture is theory AND design AND technology.

I describe designing as an activity (**translat-ing, word-ing, imagen-ing** that is situated in the triangle among primordial languages (Peter De Graeve): philosophy, science, and art on the one hand, and concepts, functions, and affects as elements of (creative) thinking on the other hand (Deleuze).

Design takes place and moves within the fields of logics, ethics, and aesthetics (Kant), and within the areas of knowledge of imagination, reason, and intuition (Spinoza). Lastly, designing is also embodied in time, space, and consciousness (Deleuze).

Inherent to human existence is a kind of endless desire (chronic desire, according to Camus) that considers surviving as living better than before, a pursuit of happiness. That desire creates a condition of idealizing, a search for the ideal, passing into a phase of ideation, of "seeing" ideas. This inevitably leads to the evaluation of those ideas in terms of value and meaning, in a kind of **a priori stadium**, and in the realm of **the intuitive**. **The ideal is existential** and places becoming above being. The orientation toward becoming (idealism, utopia), as extraction from the past and projection into the future, requires every creative activity—including, for instance, architecture—to create significance. Every human orientation toward the future is a form of being focused on (possible, renewed) sensemaking. This is essentially an activity in thinking and not (yet) in making.

Conceptualization, then, is the first step in the actualization of thinking, a reimbursement of meaning into being, thus into sign-ificance. Sign-ification is de first step to materialization: to form giving. Creating meaning (significance) and form giving (design) are activities in the modus of being. Placing becoming above being (resigning before designing) means that giving meaning to things is a specifically human potential that cannot escape the urge to translate (**word-ing, imagen-ing**). It is like a will to speak: wanting to say as sensemaking and wanting to say as expression (poiesis).

Creation (the pro-jecting, giving birth to) is a movement from becoming to being, an insertion of being into becoming. A continuous becoming, instead of a permanent being. All this sounds perhaps abstract, but it is about framing intuitive knowing within the a priori, in order to conceptualize it. Hence, a trial-and-error approach.

The term "philo-sophy" expresses this sharply: craving (philo) as a drive of the (infinite) desire, and wis-dom (sophy) as the transcending of the mere "solution." **I consider it self-evident that true (re)search for visionary development (which I label as a priori research because it prospectively**

Moon lander, seatwell, and (interior) landscape, 1979

challenges the not-yet-knowing [the intuition]), should be embedded in a real-life situation that challenges the idea(l) and allows for a posteriori research (that supports and develops a deeper knowing and self-confidence).

The investigative approach is fundamental to ground the formation of ideas and theory AND their realization and materialization.

The experiment as fundament.

Toward a conscious living...
> **"in" the world**
> **"in" society**
> a trial-and-error development of a halfway home

researching through design
> self-building as a form of self-realization

balance between settling and nomadism
but **always underway** as "backpackers" in the world
> exploring the mainland
> discovering in slow motion another world on water
> > living together with neighbors
> > plural living
> > the world as home, community as belonging
> > **ephemeral**

July 5, 2021

A BALLOON HOME (EXHIBITION VIEWS)

Filip Dujardin

A Balloon Home, exhibition (CIVA, 2021), zoom model scale 1/4

A Balloon Home, exhibition (CIVA, 2021), zoom model scale 1/4

A Balloon Home, exhibition (CIVA, 2021), zoom model scale 1/4

A Balloon Home, exhibition (CIVA, 2021), zoom model scale 1/4

A Balloon Home, exhibition (CIVA, 2021), model scale I/4

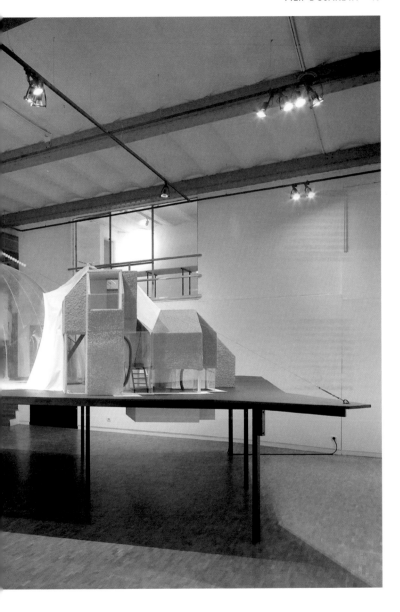

A Balloon Home, exhibition (CIVA, 2021), archive presentation

A Balloon Home, exhibition (CIVA, 2021), model scale 1/4 and slide archive presentation

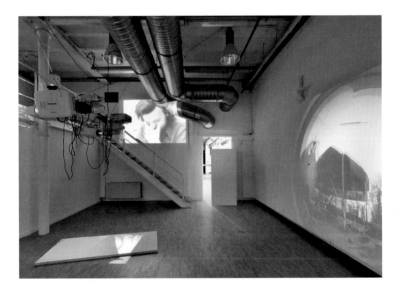

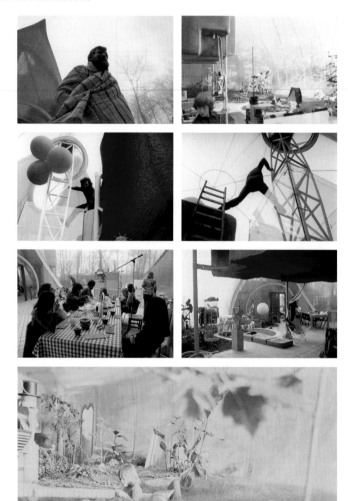

Balloon life, 1975

A TEMPORARY DATUM

Peter Swinnen & A.J. Lode Janssens

New organs of perception come into being as a result of necessity—therefore, increase your necessity so that you may increase your perception.
— Rumi

A.J. Lode Janssens   Good to see you, man! It's been such a long time.

Peter Swinnen   Nearly twenty-five years: since graduation at the Sint-Lucas School of Architecture in Brussels. You were dean, and you handed me my architecture diploma.

LJ   And now this! Are you sure you want to go through with this—the exhibition, the book, the documentary, this conversation?

PS   Your dome experiment has always intrigued me immensely, even though I lost sight of it for a while. And so little is known about it.

LJ   The project is a distant past for me. I never think about it anymore. It was an unusually personal experiment, that's for sure. It was fully completed too, very empirical—an exploration with a sliding hypothesis. The reason so little is known about it is mostly due to my aversion to publicity. I never sought it out as an architect; I hated it, and I still do. Publicity stinks.

PS   The first time, and probably also the last time, I heard something about your dome project was in 1993, about halfway through my architecture studies. You had recently become dean and gave a lecture about it. I especially remember the deafening silence after the presentation. The student audience was stupefied.

LJ   That might have been the last presentation I gave about the project. I frequently experienced those kind of silences. It was as if the public did not quite understand what truly motivated us—the radicality of testing—despite the fact that I always spoke about it.

PS   I've always read the experiment as extremely consistent, sometimes even on the verge of the uncanny.

LJ   You have to be consistent. But that does not necessarily rule out contradictions. After all, we were doing things that we had no prior knowledge of. The consequences always come after the fact. The experiment was mostly born out of a persistent dissatisfaction—my extremely critical predisposition and an unrelenting desire for analysis and understanding.

PS   What, exactly, was the experiment about for you?

LJ   Experimenting with life. An empirical residence. Housing oneself temporarily. Work-in-progress. Nomadic too—especially that. Attempting to reconcile the symbiosis between form and content, image and story, doing and thinking. As such, it was truly a pedagogical experiment, first and foremost for ourselves. We had formulated the ambition that afterward—after ten years of experimenting—we would share our findings as a commons, not as dogma, but as an example of a possible future form of living. I wanted to experience that personally, at least once.

PS   An important premise of the experiment was that you became your own client in order to operate, by necessity, outside of the regular practice and protocols of traditional architecture—to be able to consciously defy it.

LJ   I have always had a love-hate relationship with architecture.

PS   One of the documents from your archives is an A0 board that introduces the experiment (I suspect for an exhibition) that says something like: "Architect, accomplice of capitalism and the elite, parasite" and (in red caps) "I AM SICK OF IT." Why this virulent attitude?

LJ   As a profession, architecture never interested me. I have always wanted to make things that were meaningful. I needed to distance myself entirely from "design" within the discipline of architecture. I'm not at all interested in an architecture that is purely concerned with building. Just like "style," or the modernism within which I grew up—all of which were well established.

PS   Architectural form as a means to problematize.

LJ   Plus, repetition bores me! I want to be continually studying, continually questioning.

PS   Acquiring—and retaining—clients under these conditions is hardly obvious, and is more often a contradiction than anything else.

LJ   Throughout my practice, I encountered seven or eight clients who had faith in realizing a project together. Those projects, by the way, cannot be compared at all, and they can definitely not be defined by a common style. Indeed, I find the very concept of clients problematic, in the sense that it demonstrates a great belief in the architect. I've always felt uncomfortable with that—especially the fact that I used architectural commissions to question and research something, without being certain that the client truly understood that method. And I can assure you, I would speak at length with my clients, not shying away from anything—endlessly long conversations, philosophical reflections, questions, many questions... I've never really understood how clients would find me. One of them, for example, was a former student of mine. He had visited our dome and asked me to make him a residence with similar qualities. I had to convince him that I could not deliver such an experiment; it would have resulted in nothing short of disaster. But he kept pushing, so finally I forced myself to make a specific design, but no dome. It did have a large glass conservatory and a few other specific details and attachments. I baptized it the Solar House.

PS   So that project is not a refurbishment of an existing building? I always thought the brick core was an 'as found' object to which you simply added appendices; a PUR coated bedroom, a wooden garage, ...

LJ   It was not a renovation. But I admit, it was a slightly foolish architectural project.

Solar House De Decker, Alsemberg, 1979

PS   Similar to the dome project, it has a strong sense of empirical trial-and-error, testing at a one-to-one scale, without any predefined standards.

LJ   As I said, repetition fundamentally bores me. In terms of the dome project, I had no other choice than to be my own client in order to allow the real inspiration and relevant design to emerge. They were ultimately whispered to me by the 1969 moon landing—and by the womb—two primal forms of living. I was especially attracted to create a form of "de-architecturalization": how not to make any architecture. But this is definitely not anti-architecture! I sought more to create a conditioned, temporary environment. Dwelling is always temporary, no matter what. One thing was certain: the project could not be about building a house. I have something against a "house" because it represents an appropriation of the ground. You can never occupy ground. In addition to that, if you think and act from a temporary and nomadic position, what you construct does not have to last as long.

PS   Did you have any crucial references? A few weeks ago, I received a part of your archives. One thing I found among the files was an image of François Dallegret's 1965 *Environment-Bubble*.

LJ   There were quite a few experiments with plastic at the time, although mostly provocative installations and not so many realistic living environments. I barely remember Dallegret's project. I would frequently

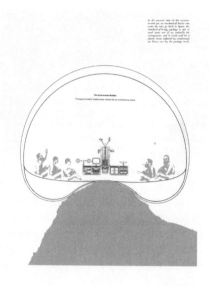

François Dallegret,
The Environment-Bubble,
from Reyner Banham,
"A Home Is Not a House,"
Art in America, April 1965

receive references from colleagues, which I would archive. Alfons Hoppenbrouwers, my passionate and erudite predecessor as dean of Sint-Lucas, often sent me things. That reference surely came from him.

In preparation for our experiment, I did visit the Internationale Kunststoffhaus Ausstellung der Welt, the IKA 71, in Lüdenscheid. On display there were self-supporting pneumatic membranes, polyester cells, and new foam technologies—projects that seemed to me like the logical continuation of the work of Raymond Loewy or Jean Prouvé, or even Ionel Schein. There was one project in particular that caught my attention: a tree hut that served to demonstrate novel polyurethane foam technology. Due to UV light it had turned a reddish color, which camouflaged it against the surrounding trees. This inspired me enormously, and I applied it throughout the parents' and children's units. That foam was of course a total contradiction, ecologically speaking. You should not assume that the dome project was consistent across the board. Underground, for example, lots of different technical installations were placed up to a depth of 4.5 meters. What kind of "house" has such machines?

Internationale Kunststoffhaus Ausstellung, 1971

PS   The very first draft you designed was extremely radical.

LJ   It was a cave dwelling, giving maximum space to nature. For that first
      draft we wanted to sculpt all the living spaces at a one-to-one scale,
      like a sand sculpture. Then, we would cover them with polyurethane,
      concrete, and a coating, and afterward, when everything was dry, we
      would remove the sand. Then, nature would take over and grow over
      everything. The sculpting followed the principles of *le négatif actif*,
      as developed by Oskar Hansen, a teaching I also used in my design
      studios at the Sint-Lucas School of Architecture.

PS   In going through the archives, I noticed how meticulously you had pre-
      pared and researched everything for the final design. If one were to lay
      out all your material sheets and technical references, the design of the
      dome with its extensions would almost appear by itself. I'm simplifying

Cave dwelling, first draft design, 1969

things, but it is remarkable how focused your work was—and how you monitored the experiment afterward like a meticulous logbook.

LJ   I spent a year and a half, from late 1969 to mid-1971, designing and collecting things. I designed the rudimentary form relatively quickly, as it was mostly dictated by the landscape. But the rest—especially the children's part—I had to keep designing to make it clearer. The children's units truly blocked me in the design process. I could not figure it out morally. To what extent can you impose a far-reaching vision of life onto children? I drew many different drafts and scenarios. The very first design consisted of a covered dock linked to the dome, provided with three small caravans, a module for every child. It was a very literal symbolism: a dock that extends away from the "mainland" and points toward the outside world, while being a place of true welcoming. You land at the dock and you are home. The idea was that every child, once they would go off to college, would be able to move elsewhere with that caravan and instantly have access to their own fetal living unit. However, it quickly became apparent that this would be too expensive—don't forget that we financed the entire experiment ourselves. Buying three caravans, while the youngest was only two years old, was just unrealistic. Plus, where would they find a terrain to station their caravans? The foundational idea had good intentions, but it went too far. Eventually, the caravans became fixed units that I could build myself. A minimal steel frame with wood and Plexiglas panels, covered with polyurethane. The idea of the personal cell, where one can retreat, nonetheless remained. It was an important compensation in relation to the absolute openness of the dome itself.

PS   The dome and the cells were really only half of the project, the more sedentary segment. The other half, the nomadic unit, was never fully realized.

LJ   The dome was indeed only part of the story. The full name of the experiment was Symbiosis & Symbicle. Symbiosis represented the dome and the cells, culture and nature, two worlds that intertwine and clash to their mutual benefit. The Symbicle, a neologism I invented, was actually the most important part of the experiment. I had

Balloon with jetty design, children's units, Humbeek, 1969, non-executed

imagined a kind of mobile home, an inflatable dome on wheels. With a diameter of about six meters, it would have the scale of a living space for a family of five. The Symbicle would allow us to travel for up to six months. I had planned to use a chassis of a Citroën H Van to mount the inflatable on. The Symbicle would dock at the dome, under the highest part of the carport tarp, next to the entrance. In the main dome, we had installed a metal loop to which an accordion sluice could be attached, similar to how an airplane is attached to a terminal. In this way, the Symbicle would become part of the dome, so we could temporarily house friends, for example. The fact that the Symbicle never became a reality was an issue of budget, but also of technology. Eventually, I had to acknowledge that I didn't have the technical capacity to build it. In the end, we replaced the nomadic part with more conventional and affordable alternatives: first, a second-hand caravan that we traveled around with for twenty years; later we bought a small boat, because a caravan cannot go across water and a big part of the world is water.

PS   Temporary residence and nomadism as one undividable nucleus.

LJ   Humans are always living by the grace of opposites. Body and mind. There is an inescapable necessity to settle and to be nomadic. What is settling? What is being a nomad? And how do you unite them? You don't have to choose one or the other. I considered the dome to be a halfway home, a minimal settlement between two points on a route, part of a shared network. In this way, nomadism is life necessity. That does not mean only traveling—you cannot be continuously nomadic. The original nomads would also temporarily settle down. I thought that balance should be revived.

PS   Can you explain the idea of the halfway home?

LJ   Did you know that the balloon could not be locked? There was no key, the door was always open—even when we traveled for longer periods of time. A halfway home is a concept that dates back to the time when traveling was more than a one-day affair, and a short stay

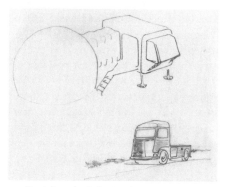

Sketch design for the Symbicle (never realized), 1970

along the way was necessary. A home halfway on the trip. That's why the dome was intentionally a temporary residence that desired to be somewhere halfway, always available if needed. We assumed that if we were traveling, someone else within our social circle would make use of the halfway home. And we would be using someone else's halfway home. Living instead of sedentary dwelling. They would be in motion; we would be in motion.

PS   How did you decide, within your de-architectural spatial language, the dimensions of spaces and atmospheres—especially for the typical dwelling functions?

LJ   The air-supported dome, which had a diameter of fourteen meters, was primarily defined by the available space on the parcel, the space free of vegetation. The project was largely determined by that capricious shape between the existing nature and the structure. The height of the dome resulted from the scale of the so-called moon lander, the parents' unit that I conceptualized as a kind of Lunar Excursion Module cell. I saw it as a mobile volume that could be positioned in different ways, making different arrangements possible. The scale of the tent structure on the east side, which sheltered the entrance and carport, had to be big enough to offer the required protection. The children's units on the southwest side were compact cells, tailored to the individual. The rest was free space, in unity with the landscape.

PS   The tensile canvas structures required special attention.

LJ   We cut them ourselves. I had experimented quite a bit with canvas structures and their tensile logic in my previous architectural practice, Atelier Alpha, together with Willy Van Der Meeren. One of our more interesting experiments was the construction of our own studio space. The first canvas was cut too straight and flew off with the first storm. I think we had to recut it at least three times until we finally found a logical, natural shape. Making a tensile canvas is a matter of cut. It's as simple as that—or, as difficult as that.

PS   For the dome, two canvasses were designed and installed.

Atelier Alpha, first tent structure, 1966   Atelier Alpha, final tent structure, 1967

LJ   We used nonflammable Trevira fabrics. The tarp over the carport entrance was an effective tent structure that was also intended to protect the dome against weathering and storms. But the kids' tent was not a real tensile structure; it was, rather, an example of what I call the "handkerchief principle." During lectures, I frequently invited two people from the audience to tightly hold two corners of a handkerchief and pull hard. Then, I would push down in the middle with one finger, effortlessly, as if there was no tension at all. The kids' tent was mostly needed as a mental transition zone between the dome and the their private cells.

PS   The project was a continuous series, or even an interpenetration, of transitionary atmospheres, with extremely thin partitions. Not a simple question of inside or outside.

LJ   It was an intrinsic whole of threshold zones, transitions, overlaps, and marginal areas—with the dome at its heart, which was materialized in ribbed and welded, transparent, extremely thin, non-fiber–reinforced and inflammable eltexyl PVC foil. Regardless of how minimal it was, an entirely transparent membrane could not prevent nature from turning into "culture" inside. The desire to cancel inside and outside, however, was definitely present. In the second edition of the Design Biënnale Interieur in Kortrijk, in 1970, I heard two lectures that left a strong impression on me. Aldo Van Eyck spoke about his concept of thresholds, and the "ecotect" Louis Le Roy proposed that you simply have to guide nature. I was not necessarily interested in what they both designed, but how they talked about it. That's why we let nature continue to grow. And we didn't plant any trees in places where there weren't any. One tree appeared to be blocking the way during the construction, an oak, so we let it remain inside the children's tent. Of course, it did not survive. An oak is not made to grow inside. Inside the dome, though, several shrubs continued to grow lush. Once we were gifted a poinsettia and it grew to be four meters tall!

PS   Moss covered the PVC dome quite quickly, and it hardened from due to the light.

LJ   Indeed. We would make new "windows" by cleaning away circles of moss. Over time, after six or seven years, the dome became a more enclosed interior space due to the moss. And that's without even considering the impact of the weather. Snow became a negative thing in our experience. Philosophically speaking, I thought that it would be beautiful—crystals letting through light. But in reality, it was grizzled, gray, and sad. Clearly, the plastic had its limits even though we managed to push those them considerably.

An anecdote: One day a shiny black Mercedes pulled into our driveway unannounced. Several fancy gentlemen got out and introduced themselves as representatives of Bayer, the German chemical giant. They knew a lot more about plastic than I did. With tooth and nail they tried to communicate to us that what we were doing was essentially impossible. Such a thin foil, seven meters high, fourteen meters wide—it should have ripped a long time ago, they claimed. What did occur was that the elasticity of the PVC was much greater than predicted. The low air pressure inside was just enough to maintain its shape. However, due to the large scale of the structure, the foil kept expanding. Instead of the predicted 1 percent, it stretched about 7 percent. At some point, we installed a mesh of steel cables, covered with transparent nylon, across the PVC foil. The dome would have otherwise touched the cables and part of the canvas, which could have led to damage.

Dome with and without safety net, 1975–76

PS   An improvisation out of necessity.

LJ   It did not bother me in the least. Other people had more difficulty
      with it. Everyone seemed to have an opinion as to what the experi-
      ment was about. Many people were convinced it was a far-reaching
      technological experiment. But that is just ridiculous. It was totally
      handcrafted. Others saw it purely as form, as if I wanted to prove
      what the future would look like. Then there were those who thought
      I was preoccupied with ecological architecture, because of how we
      lived in and with nature. Although I used certain ecological terms,
      I did not actually know anything about ecology. The main principle
      was that we needed to be able to realize it ourselves. Self-building was
      the most important principle of the experiment.

PS   Moreover, it was far from energy efficient.

LJ   The project was 100 percent dependent upon technology. There was
      an air-pressure system that required the hot-air apparatus to be on
      at all times. Electronic systems served as a back-up for any potential
      power defect that could happen. While we had not planned for this
      initially, we learned the hard way that it was necessary—after our first
      blackout. The dome needed to have an automatic emergency switch.
      A continuous measuring of wind speed ensured the correct indoor air
      pressure. In case of a storm or snow, we temporarily increased the pres-
      sure. In terms of heating, the insulation value of the dome was zero.

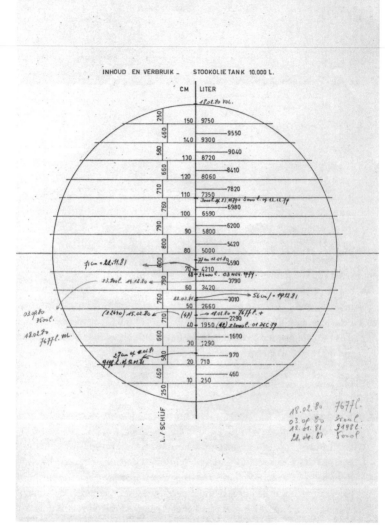

Balloon oil consumption log, 1982

Overall, we ascertained that we had more heat recovery than heat loss, thanks to the greenhouse effect. During winter there were a few very intense moments when we were really at the limit, about 15 degrees inside. If the weather had been colder, we would not have been able to warm the dome any longer. All in all, the cost and quantity of fuel for heating was exceptionally high. We consumed about 15,000 liters per year, about two or three times the consumption of a regular household.

PS   The project costs totaled around 50,000 euros, which was not cheap at the time, of which 40 percent went to heating costs. It was an expensive experiment in other respects as well—mentally, too.

LJ   I feel like I did what I had to do. In the end, we effectively spent the equivalent of the price of a "good house." At the time, I built several houses for less than half of the cost of the dome. The radical nature of the experiment itself—a decade of living and working under the open sky—took its toll psychologically. We kept trying to live our lives as normally as possible, attempting to achieve the conceivable maximum. Though this didn't take into account the effect the external world would have on us. Trauma was caused especially by the unsolicited erasure of the boundaries between public and private.

PS   Shielding off was literally impossible.

LJ   At all possible and impossible moments, people would come to take a look at the strange balloon. Any consideration of the site as a residential family home was lacking. People could literally walk in anytime. It frequently happened that when we were away the whole thing would collapse due to unregulated pressure, because people would often forget to simply close the door behind them. At times, a bus with thirty people would stop and they would all stand there, peering inside. I never anticipated any of this. All in all, I suspect we had over 2,000 visitors, most of them unannounced. This really had a psychological impact on me. Ever since, I have consciously retracted from public life as much as possible.

PS   For students, however, it appears you would gladly make an exception.

LJ   Yes. Although I never used the dome directly in my educational en-
      deavors, I never refused to share information about it and I would
      allow students, if they asked, to experience it for themselves. After all,
      I lived for my students. I considered it my duty to transmit the story
      that my family and I were learning every day. Why else undertake
      such a project? There was not a school in the country that did not
      send a delegation. Many professors and their assistants also visited.
      As long as I felt their interest was genuine, and they were not just
      there to be nosy, I didn't mind at all. At some point, Geert Bekaert was
      drawn to the project; it took hold of him. He included it in the classes
      he taught at the Department of Architecture and Planning in Leuven,
      and he invited me to speak about the experiment on several occasions.
      We had a mutual appreciation of each other's work, although we could
      not be further apart in our approach to life. This is how it came about
      that Bekaert, in collaboration with with filmmaker Jef Cornelis, whom
      I greatly respected, made a documentary for national television about
      the experiment. Unfortunately, I don't think there is a copy left of it.

PS   Video documentation would indeed have been insightful material,
      even if it had just been to show how many times the project shape-
      shifted due to repair work, optimizations, wear and tear, the seasons,
      birds picking at the polyurethane of the kids' units... From 1980
      onward, you slowly started intentionally rebuilding the interior of the
      dome. It was a projection of your forthcoming residence, as a kind of
      wooden model at a one-to-one scale.

LJ   The plastic foil was not going to last longer than ten years. And I had
      to guarantee shelter for my family. So, we gradually started with an
      in-between experiment: the building of a temporary Winter house
      inside the dome, for which we simply enclosed the kitchen with sheet
      material in order to create an intermediate climate. From this, the
      plan for a post-dome dwelling emerged, without putting it on paper
      beforehand. An improvised metamorphosis.

PS   It is remarkable that you remained on the same site. A site, moreover,
      located in your native village, although it could have been anywhere
      in terms of temporary dwelling.

The Winter house, 1980

LJ   The location was not important. I was born there, but I did not have any relationship whatsoever to that liberal, traditionalist village. The only thing that mattered was that the site was not visible from the street. Otherwise, we would never have been able, or allowed, to experiment there. Actually, this also became clear during the difficult permit application process. We never received a building permit, only a temporary, ten-year permit to experiment. We ended up staying longer, simply because it was a place where we could play and build and live uninhibited, without leaving any real physical traces.

PS   Back to the wooden metamorphosis. The process of "building from within" was brutally interrupted in February 1982 when the dome suddenly collapsed.

LJ   Despite the fact that we had the necessary equipment to neutralize sudden snowfall, that night there had been a "silent" snowfall, without wind or storm. That's why the equipment faltered. When we woke up, we saw a huge dent in the dome. In a panicked reaction I tried to shove the snow off from the inside, but due to the shift of snow mass, the foil suddenly gave out. The collapse happened in a really unfortunate moment, because I had planned to dismantle the dome the following Summer. I had a clear plan to take a knife and cut away the balloon, then take a few A4 samples—one from each cardinal direction—and have them analyzed in a laboratory, as part of the emperical ten year experiment. The snow beat me to it, and suddenly we didn't have an adequate home, even though part of the wooden structure was already built. We accelerated the building of the new residence and in the end we managed. We continued to live there until 2000, and sold it in 2003. We really wanted to leave at that point. Again, that nomadic urge.

PS   At the beginning of our conversation, you expressed your concern about the children, and how they would all experience this. How do you think this experiment was for them?

Second house, 1983–2003

LJ   The dome and garden were clearly a playground paradise. Such a free space where everything was possible, utterly uninhibited and free. On top of that, they had their own private cells and a separate tent. I suspect they had difficult moments, especially when there was bad weather. When there was hail, snow, or an unexpected cloudburst, everything was experienced at double intensity inside the dome. In these moments, we were always alert. The kids would then quickly go to their own little units. To be honest, the children never mentioned what they truly thought of this experiment.

PS   Not even when they grew up and had a certain distance from the experience?

LJ   No. They never really revealed their experience or memories. As if it was not necessary to talk about it. Or maybe because they didn't know how to talk about it. Strictly speaking, I don't know what to think about the experiment and its effects. Was it a problem? Was it livable? Did it cause certain traumas?

PS   Did you ever ask them those questions yourself?

LJ   No. I never really had the courage to bring it up, because I wouldn't like to hear them suddenly tell me that the experiment is a primary source of trauma or problems in their lives. After all those years I am still worried about that. The pressure inside the dome for example, no matter how weak it was, was it not harmful to them? As grown ups we did not feel any effect, but still... In the end, it indisputably turned out to be an ideological and pedagogical project. Moreover, if you undertake such an extreme experiment, you expose your-self as a pedagogue, within the family, toward the outside world. I have always had the feeling that I was more of a pedagogue than an architect; a thinker about what it is to "de-sign." What is an idea? One simply cannot resist certain things, because they are concerned with intuition—things we already implicitly know but still need to recog-nize for what they are, disregarding notions of failure or success. An empirical execution. Pedagogically, I have been able to transmit and pass on that insight.

Imploded Balloon, February 1982

THE END OF THE FUTURE

Bart Decroos

"When your house contains such a complex of piping, flues, ducts, wires, lights, inlets, outlets, ovens, sinks, refuse disposers, hi-fi reverberators, antennae, conduits, freezers, heaters—when it contains so many services that the hardware could stand up by itself without any assistance from the house, why have a house to hold it up?"[1] With this provocation, the British architecture historian Reyner Banham opened his 1965 essay "A Home Is Not A House," but it could just as well have been a description of the so-called Balloon by Belgian architect and educator A.J. Lode Janssens. From 1973 to 1982, Janssens and his family built and lived in a pneumatic dwelling that largely consisted of only such utilities, without any house to hold them up—the only roof above their heads was an inflatable dome.

Today, there is a resurgence of interest in utopian architectural experiments of the 1960s and 1970s, made evident by recent issues of major journals and various books on the topic (the present catalogue and accompanying exhibition being one such example). But why? What conditions in contemporary architecture prompt us to look back with fascination to these technological experiments of the past? And what can they tell us?

Aside from the perhaps obvious, yet ultimately metaphorical, comparisons with the global situation of the previous year, in which the world faced a pandemic that forced people around the world to retreat into their private "bubbles," Janssens' Balloon and others' inflatable experiments strike a chord with fundamental technological developments of these first decades of the twenty-first century. Whatever the reasons may be—the omnipresence of high-tech installations in our continuously air-conditioned interiors, the onset of a second Space Age, or a fundamental crisis in modernity, among other things—we must be careful not to simply project such historical cases onto our current-day situation. Instead, we might even need to turn things upside down, "topsy turvy" as Alice would say, since global conditions have gone down a rabbit hole of crises without end, contradicting most everything we once seemed to believe. While the high-tech architecture exemplified in Janssens' Balloon might have once held the promise of a better future, perhaps today it is exactly the "future" that we need to rid ourselves of.

High-Tech Architecture

As the above quote already suggests, Banham would become one of the main champions of such early high-tech experiments. According to him, the technological progress of modern society was of the utmost importance for architecture, yet, at the same time, it also announced the demise of architecture as we knew it. At the end of his first extended study of the history of modern architecture, in 1960, he concluded:

It may well be that what we have hitherto understood as architecture, and what we are beginning to understand of technology, are incompatible disciplines. The architect who proposes to run with technology knows now that he will be in fast company, and that, in order to keep up, he may have to emulate the Futurists and discard his whole cultural load, including the professional garments by which he is recognized as an architect. If on the other hand, he decides not to do this, he may find that a technological culture has decided to go on without him.[2]

While Banham, in his typical contrarian fashion, prided himself on changing his mind multiple times throughout his career, there is nonetheless a clear direction in which he would explore the relation between architecture and technology after 1960. In "A Home Is Not A House," he described this relation as follows: "Man started with two basic ways of controlling environment: one by avoiding the issue and hiding under a rock, tree, tent or roof (this led ultimately to architecture as we know it) and the other by actually interfering with the local meteorology, usually by means of a campfire, which, in a more polished form, might lead to the kind of situation now under discussion."[3] The situation under discussion being the possibility of pneumatic architecture. From this perspective, Janssens' Balloon can be understood as such a technologically enhanced campfire: the delineation of a tempered zone, a bubble of heated air to make an otherwise inhospitable environment habitable, but without the "inefficient, unreliable, smoky" characteristics of a fire.[4]

For Banham, the rapid development of building technologies at the time seemed to hold the promise of an "other modern architecture,"[5] one that had little to do with the stylistic orthodoxy of the International Style, but instead embodied a cultural impetus that placed the machine in a privileged position within society and artistic production. In the 1960s, Banham found such architectural experiments mainly in the work of Archigram; but by the 1980s, he became increasingly drawn to the high-tech architecture of (early) Renzo Piano, Richard Rogers, and Norman Foster. Despite its generic meaning in popular culture, Banham understood the notion of high-tech as that which "offers the explicit promise, and hopefully the physical delivery, of superior environmental performance."[6] And while the delivery of such a promise relied on technological progress, high-tech was first and foremost a matter of architecture: "High Tech has far more to do with architecture than it does with Technology, even though it would be inconceivable without the availability of certain materials and techniques and the example and vital contributions of certain engineers."[7]

Yet Banham's work on high-tech architecture appeared to have been a rearguard battle. While the radical visions of early high-tech architects eventually fused with corporate aesthetics, the Western architectural culture of the late twentieth century increasingly withdrew itself into its own autonomy, suspicious of "solving" any problems external to architecture, as high-tech had promised to do. At the turn of the twenty-first century, however, the resurgence of interest in the high-tech experiments of the 1960s and 1970s seems to indicate a new-found appreciation of an architecture that solves problems, perhaps not unrelated to the various global crises that are only just erupting.

Cutting grass, inside the Balloon, 1974

A Space Odyssey

In 1968, Stanley Kubrick's *2001: A Space Odyssey* was released in theaters worldwide, receiving both ecstatic praise and outraged criticism. While the special effects and production qualities were considered to be extraordinary, there was widespread confusion on what the film was actually about. The film traces the discovery of a mysterious black monolith, first by ape-like beings in prehistoric Africa, then by astronauts at a US lunar outpost, and finally by a North American scientist in orbit around Jupiter. While the connections between these events is never explicitly addressed, the last part of the movie presents the viewer with an LSD-fueled trip in outer space, viewed through the eyes of the scientist, who, after a detour through a neoclassical bedroom where the black monolith makes a final appearance, ends up as a planet-sized fetus suspended in space next to Earth. Despite the apparent lunacy of the script, the film arrived at exactly the right time.

Just one year later, in 1969, the Space Race between the United States and the Soviet Union reached its apotheosis when US astronauts set foot on the surface of the Moon. The event was broadcasted on various news channels around the world and was hailed as the "greatest single broadcast in television history,"[8] with over 650 million viewers worldwide. The crewed Moon landing fulfilled the promise of technological progress—the dream that anything was possible—and permeated deep into the cultural consciousness of the time. In the optimistic but naive words of Banham: "Our accession to almost unlimited supplies of energy is balanced against the possibility of making our planet uninhabitable, but this again is balanced, as we stand at the threshold of space, by the growing possibility of quitting our island earth and letting down roots elsewhere."[9]

The dream, however, was short-lived

In 1972, only three years later, the United States conducted the sixth and, until today, last crewed mission to the Moon. That same year, the Club of Rome published its *Limits to Growth* report, a wake-up call for those who were still dreaming of limitless expansion. Rather symbolically, in 1973, the United States, as well as most other Western countries, faced an unprecedented oil crisis: the exploration of space had only just begun, yet they had already run out of fuel.

In hindsight, *2001: A Space Odyssey* can be interpreted as a story of humankind's technological progress: the black monolith represents the transition from one stage to another, from Earth-bound hominoids to interstellar space travelers, with the LSD trip at the end as a symbol for the presumed expansion of our consciousness that accompanies it. Yet, the final image of the "starchild" reminds us of the planet on which we were born, our so-called Mother Earth, and which, perhaps, we can never truly leave.

Bursting the Bubble

If Janssens' Balloon resembled a spaceship, its mission was to land on planet Earth—more precisely, in the small village of Humbeek, hidden away in the Belgian countryside outside of Brussels. Janssens might as well have been referring to *2001: A Space Odyssey* when he said: "In the end, the real inspiration for the Balloon came from the moon landing. And the uterus."[10]

Officially titled Symbiosis,[11] Janssens' experiment envisioned a "pressurized dome, under an extremely low pressure (1.47 mbar), with a 'moon lander' inside as a central volume and trailer-like mobile units for the children."[12] Despite its succinct technological outlook, however, the reality turned out to be quite messy. The fourteen-meter-diameter balloon, for example, was made using transparent plastic, but became overgrown with moss, undermining its ephemeral appearance. This ephemerality was already questionable from the start, since the balloon only stayed inflated thanks to an extended network of ventilation ducts and technical installations buried deep underground. In addition, the mobile units for the children, for when they would leave the "uterus" of the parental home, were never built, but instead evolved into "capsules" constructed out of plywood and coated with insulation foam, which birds ate apart shortly after their construction.

The project seems to have been riddled with contradictions: its high-tech architecture was revealed to be rudimentary and improvised. Janssens later stated: "A lot of people thought it was a technological experiment, but that is just plainly ridiculous. It was pure craftsmanship."[13] While this might sound like a counterintuitive reflection, Banham indeed affirms such contradiction: "Contrariwise, some of the most visually elaborated and highly finished works of High-Tech Architecture have, in fact, no more than a rhetorical or mythological connection with any advanced technology or engineering."[14]

While one could indeed doubt the "superior environmental performance" of the Balloon—especially given the enormous consumption of fuel that was necessary to keep it inflated and heated all year round—more fundamentally, the dwelling embodied the Space Age mythology of the time as an architectural translation of technological progress into social narrative.

In 1982, nine years after it was built, on a Winter morning, Janssens and his family woke up to find the balloon quasi collapsed under the weight of an overnight snowfall. While the experiment was only planned to last for ten years due to permit complications, the bubble nonetheless burst unexpectedly early, revealing perhaps the most fundamental insight into Banham's "technological society." As the cultural theorist Paul Virilio succinctly stated: "When you invent the ship, you also invent the shipwreck."[15] Or, more elaborately: "Every technology carries its own negativity, which is invented at the same time as technological progress."[16]

High-Tech Romanticism

In 1975, while living in the Balloon, Janssens wrote a short poem on the project. The imagery of the text not only renders clearly Janssens' intentions, it also expresses a more widespread sentiment that could be found in much of the utopian architectural experiments of the time: a return to nature—or, symbiosis. As such, the poem is structured around a metaphor of so-called organic existence, found in the following lines:

> not a building
> dead weight
> that parasites on holy ground
>
> A body
> with skin and intestines
> with heart and soul.[17]

These lines imagine a metaphor for the dwelling, not as "dead weight" on the "holy ground" of the Earth, but as a living body, part of natural life. To realize this, Janssens had to dispense with architecture as such, and aspire to the construction of an "non-architecture": "I have something against 'a house,' because it represents an anchoring, an appropriation of the soil. [...] In the end, I was mainly interested in forms of 'de-architecturalization,' in 'not making architecture.'"[18]

This ideal of a return to nature, unspoiled by human activities, can be traced back to the Romanticism of the nineteenth century (if not earlier), in response to the industrialization at the time. As John Ruskin, perhaps the first environmentalist of the modern period, wrote in 1860: "Wherever I look or travel in England or abroad, I see that men, wherever they can reach, destroy all beauty. They seem to have no other desire or hope but to have large houses and to be able to move fast. Every perfect and lovely spot which they can touch, they defile."[19] While the artistic expressions of the Romantic period are often understood as an expression of the desire to return to nature, they are simultaneously the symptom of the opposite: a definitive rupture between the human space of culture and the nonhuman space of nature, organized through the apparatuses of industrial exploitation. The presumed "return" of Romanticism was instead the construction of an idyllic "nature" that had not existed before. As the theorist Timothy Morton writes, "Nature, practically a synonym for evil in the Middle Ages, was considered the basis for social good by the Romantic period."[20]

While nineteenth-century Romanticism envisioned a return to nature as an escape from and antidote to the destruction and pollution of industrialization, during the 1970s, in the middle of that confrontation between the

WERKGEMEENSCHAP WARD DE NEYS EN A.J. LODE JANSSENS KONINKLIJKE SINTE MARIASTRAAT 72
1030 BRUSSEL-BELGIE TELEFOON 02/15.26.90 POSTCHECKREKENING 8950.04 B.T.W. 548.211.732

een STRUKTUUR

organiek bestaan
leven
en zich in stand houden
door inwendig evenwicht van krachten
spel van aktie en reaktie
spanning.

      geen gebouw
      dood gewicht
      dat parasiteert op heilige bodem

Een lichaam
met huid en ingewanden
met hart en ziel.

een huid als een spannend omhulsel
vezel-versterkt ;
kabels, als spieren om zich te rechten

ingewanden (ondergronds-binnenshuids)
organen en kanalen
die het vel modeleren
elektronics zenuwstelsel
dat impulsen stuurt
regelt.

Wij,
   een ziel
   in ons 'grote' lichaam

wij zijn.

            Lode
            06.05.75

limitless expansion of Space Age mythology and the limits to growth imposed by a newfound environmentalism, such a return to nature was imagined precisely through technology. In Janssens' poem, this tension becomes visible in the final stanza, as a fusion of the organic with the mechanical:

> organs and canals
> that model the skin
> electronic nerve system
> that sends out impulses
> regulates.[21]

Où atterir?

In 1972, another sci-fi film was released: *Silent Running*. The film was the directorial debut of Douglas Trumbull, the special effects supervisor on Kubrick's film, though its narrative significantly diverted from the Space Age mythology found in Kubrick.

The story takes place in an undefined future, at a time when all plant life on Earth has gone extinct. The entire surface of the planet has been covered with an undefined but all-encompassing interior—a planet-scale balloon, one might imagine—which is permanently air-conditioned at room temperature. The film is set, however, on board the Valley Forge, part of a fleet of American Airlines space freighters that are orbiting Saturn. Each of the freighters is equipped with large, geodesic domes—that other type of bubble architecture—in which fragments of various types of landscapes that are now lost on Earth have been conserved. The film begins when the crew of the Valley Forge receives an order to dump and destroy these remnants of natural life: the ships are needed for commercial travel and, in a technologically-advanced future, who needs "wild nature" anyway? *Silent Running* presents us with an inverted view of the Space Age mythology: it is not humankind that encloses itself in capsular constructions to conquer space, rather it is nature that is launched into orbit, while humankind stays behind and transforms Earth into a continuous and controlled interior, undoubtedly of "superior environmental performance."

In his 2017 pamphlet on climate politics titled *Où atterir?* (translated into English as *Down to Earth*), the sociologist Bruno Latour describes the basic conflict underlying modernity in terms of a struggle between the global and the local: "There is no Earth corresponding to the infinite horizon of the Global, but at the same time the Local is much too narrow, too shrunken, to accommodate the multiplicity of beings belonging to the terrestrial world."[22] We have reached for the stars, but upon returning, found that there is no Earth to return to—so where can we still land?

Modernity responds with an all-too-cynical answer—the simple inversion of Space Age mythology: more of the same. Since the turn of the twenty-first century, we have seen the advent of a second Space Race, yet this time it is not governmental agencies supposedly striving for the common good, but billionaire-controlled multinational companies such as Elon Musk's SpaceX, Richard Branson's Virgin Galactic, or Jeff Bezos's Blue Origin, who are in a tight race to Mars and beyond. But while the first Space Race might still have had the dream of bringing humankind to the stars, the goal of these companies is rather commercial, including, among other things, mining operations on mineral-rich asteroids—a revival of the imperialist ideology that ventures into a supposedly terra nullis only to return with extracted resources, justified as a lifeline for a dying planet.[23]

The End of the Future

The irony is perhaps that this inverted Space Age mythology relies on the same functionalist logic found in the kind of environmentalism that resulted in the *Limits to Growth report*: a worldview that considers "nature," whether on this planet or another, as an economic externality full of inert resources upon which our human society is built. Such a logic was further developed in the *Our Common Future report of the United Nation's Brundtland Commission*, published in 1987, which launched the paradigm of sustainability. In contrast to the idyllic nature of the Romantic period, here nature became a calculation of costs and benefits, and a question of how far we can push things before they start to break down. As Timothy Morton puts it: "What exactly are we sustaining when we talk about sustainability? An intrinsically out-of-control system that sucks in grey goo at one end and pushes out grey value at the other."[24]

Driven by the paradigm of sustainability, the field of architecture has witnessed an explosion of increasingly advanced building technologies, solutions intended to mitigate the quantified impact of the construction industry on the environment, all the while sustaining our desire "to have large houses and to be able to move fast." Such sustainable building technologies have become omnipresent, however, until now, the industry standard has been to hide them: in cavity walls, in suspended ceilings and raised floors, underground, or covered by green roofs. The architectural practice of the twenty-first century has yet to catch up with the "fast company" of such technologies, which returns us to Banham's plea for a truly technological culture.

For Banham, the pioneers of such a technological culture were undoubtedly the Futurists, who, at the turn of the twentieth century, had managed to accept the presence of machines on their own terms. Moreover, the Futurists had completely embraced the idea that technology is in a state of continual change. One of the most radical propositions in "Manifesto of Futurist Architecture" from 1914 was the assertion that the "fundamental characteristics of Futurist architecture will be obsolescence and transience. Houses will last less long than we. Each generation will have to build its own city."[25]

In other words, for the Futurists as well as for Banham, technology was there to make the future happen. Today, within the paradigm of sustainability, technology is there to prevent the future from happening.

Janssens' Balloon, and many of the other utopian architectural experiments of the 1960s and 1970s, reminds us of a moment in history when technology was not yet constrained by the conservative agenda of sustainability, but instead still held the utopian promise for imagining and constructing a different world. To do so today, we might have to rethink what role technology still can play, especially, and perhaps most importantly, outside of modern discourses on the "future."

1 Reyner Banham, "A Home Is Not A House," *Art in America* 2 (1965): 70.

2 Reyner Banham, *Theory and Design in the First Machine Age* (London: Architectural Press, 1960), 329–30.

3 Banham, "A Home Is Not A House," 75.

4 Ibid.

5 Reyner Banham, "High Tech and Advanced Engineering" (ca. 1987), in Todd Gannon, *Reyner Banham and the Paradoxes of High Tech* (Los Angeles: Getty Research Institute, 2017), 243.

6 Ibid., 244.

7 Ibid., 237.

8 Robert Wussler in Steve Knoll, "First Man on the Moon Has TV Networks in Orbit," *Variety*, July 16, 1969. Wussler was the executive producer of CBS's coverage of the event.

9 Banham, *Theory and Design in the First Machine Age*, 9.

10 A.J. Lode Janssens in Peter Swinnen, "Werken aan het plafond, A.J. Lode Janssens," *HART Magazine*, February 3, 2021, https://hart-magazine.be/artikels/de-ongevraagde-architect-deel-3-5; my translation.

11 Initially, the full title of the experiment was Symbiosis & Symbicle, which referred to the house (Symbiosis) and a mobile balloon unit (Symbicle). Because the latter was never realized, the current text addresses only the former.

12 Janssens in Swinnen, "Werken aan het plafond, A.J. Lode Janssens."

13 Ibid.

14 Banham, "High Tech and Advanced Engineering," 240.

15 Paul Virilio, *Politics of the Very Worst*, trans. Michael Cavaliere (New York: Semiotext[e], 1999), 89.

16 Ibid.

17 A.J. Lode Janssens, "Schrijfsel," unpublished, 1975; my translation.

18 Janssens in Swinnen, "Werken aan het plafond, A.J. Lode Janssens."

19 John Ruskin, "The Hesperid Aeglé" (1860), in *Selected Writings*, ed. Dinah Birch (Oxford: Oxford University Press, 2009), 136.

20 Timothy Morton, *Ecology without Nature: Rethinking Environmental Aesthetics* (Cambridge, MA: Harvard University Press, 2007), 15.

21 Janssens, "Schrijfsel."

22 Bruno Latour, *Down to Earth: Politics in the New Climatic Regime*, trans. Catherine Porter (Cambridge: Polity Press, 2018), 69.

23 In 2020, SpaceX won the launch contract for NASA's 2022 mission to explore the mineral-rich asteroid 16 Psyche: "NASA and SpaceX Mission to Find Space Gold," *BBC*, March 12, 2020, https://www.bbc.co.uk/newsround/51858259.

24 Timothy Morton, *Hyperobjects: Philosophy and Ecology after the End of the World* (Minneapolis: University of Minnesota Press, 2013), 113.

25 Antonio Sant'Elia, "Manifesto of Futurist Architecture" (1914), in *Programs and Manifestoes on 20th-Century Architecture*, ed. Ulrich Conrads (Cambridge MA: MIT Press, 1970), 36.

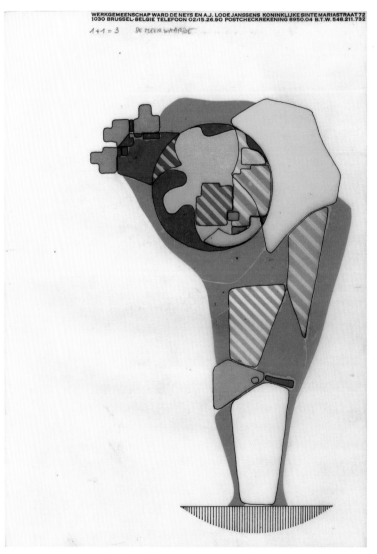

WERKGEMEENSCHAP WARD DE NEYS EN A.J. LODE JANSSENS KONINKLIJKE SINTE MARIASTRAAT 72
1030 BRUSSEL-BELGIE TELEFOON 02/15.26.90 POSTCHECKREKENING 8950.04 B.T.W. 548.211.732

1+1 = 3   DE MEERWAARDE

Symbiosis & Symbicle, treshold diagram, 1970

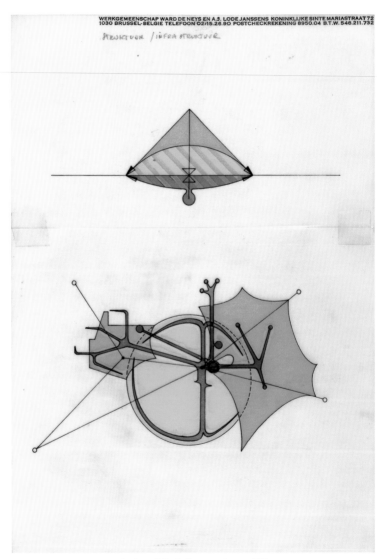

Symbiosis & Symbicle, zoning diagram, 1970

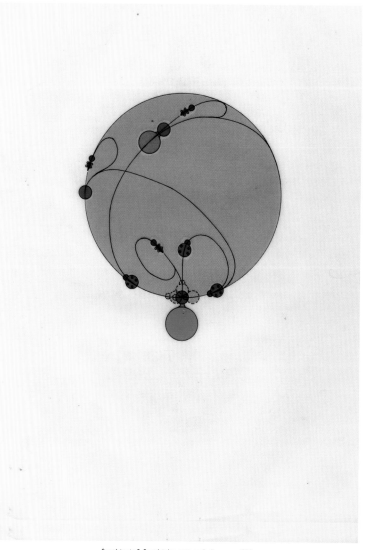

Symbiosis & Symbicle, network diagram, 1970

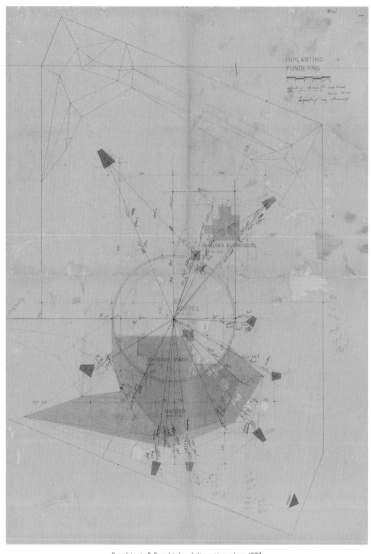

Symbiosis & Symbicle, delineation plan, 1973

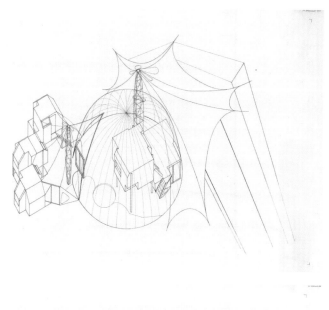

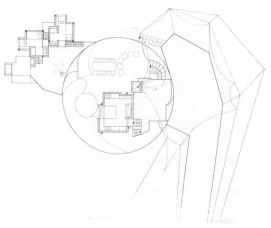

Symbiosis & Symbicle, plan & axonometric drawing, 1972

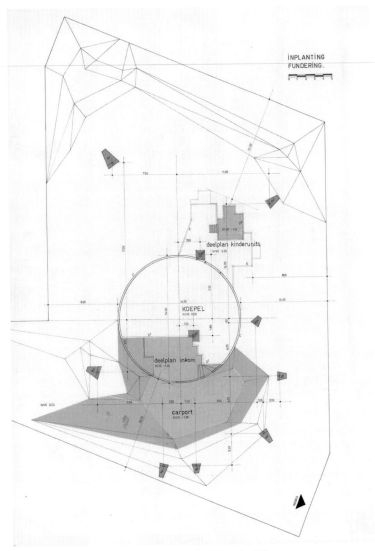

Symbiosis & Symbicle, foundation plan, 1972

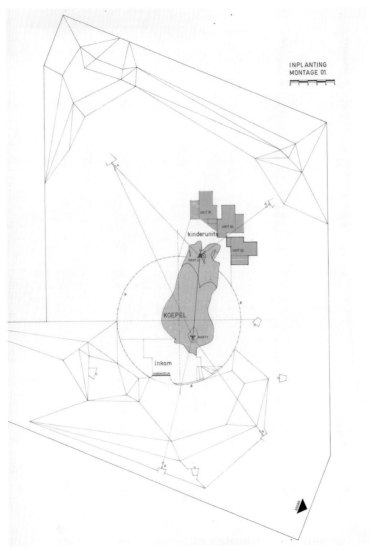

Symbiosis & Symbicle, montage phase 01, 1972

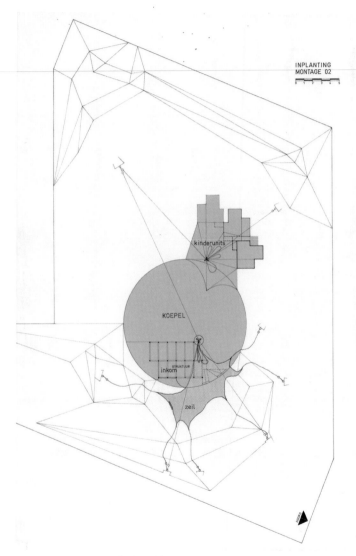

Symbiosis & Symbicle, montage phase 02, 1972

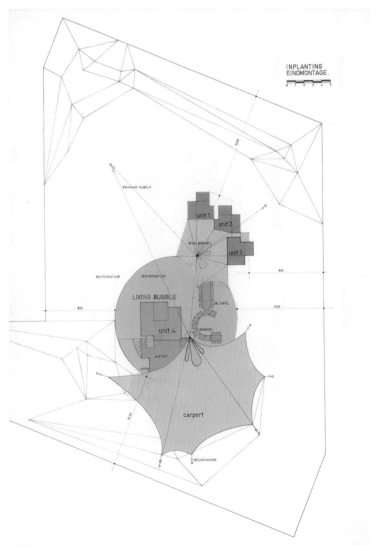

Symbiosis & Symbicle, final montage phase, 1972

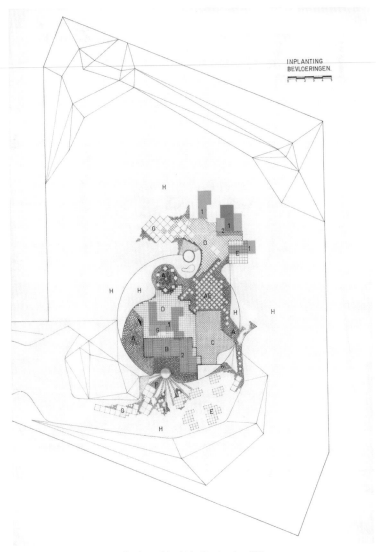

Symbiosis & Symbicle, flooring plan, 1972

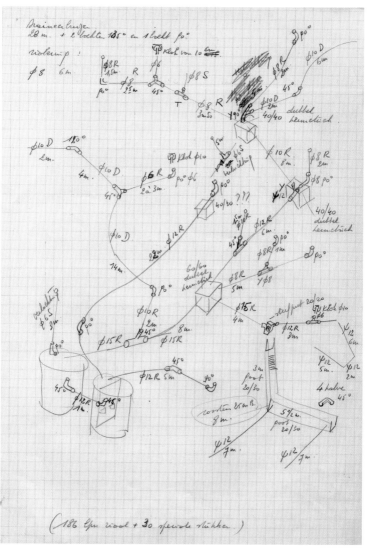

Symbiosis & Symbicle, draining and sewage scheme, 1972

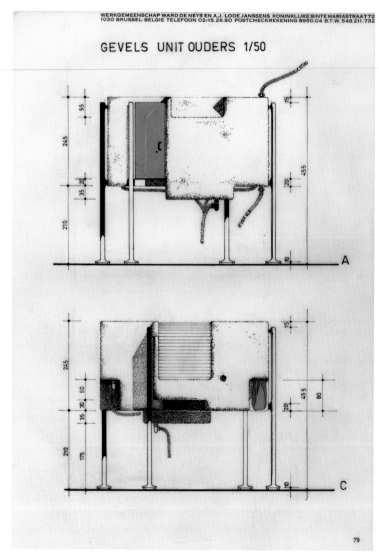

Symbiosis & Symbicle, parents' unit ('Moon Lander'), 1972

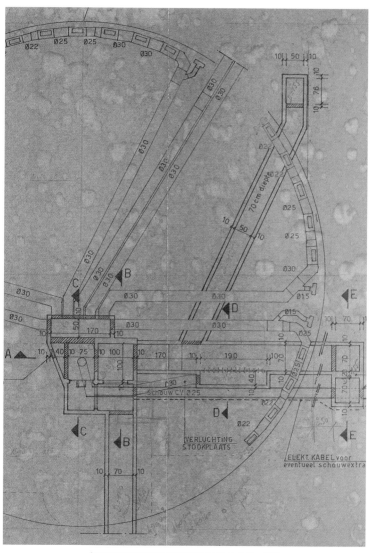

Symbiosis & Symbicle, detail technical installation, 1972

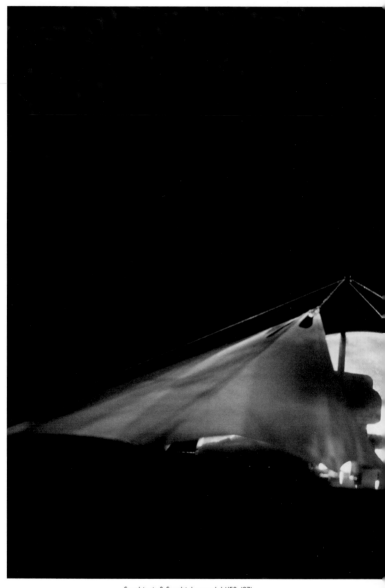

Symbiosis & Symbicle, model 1/50, 1971

Symbiosis & Symbicle, street access with tubular mailbox, 1976

Symbiosis & Symbicle, construction site / steel structures children's units, 1973

Symbiosis & Symbicle, construction site / steel structure parents' unit / air vents, 1973

Symbiosis & Symbicle, the dome without air pressure, 1973

Symbiosis & Symbicle, the air-pressured dome, 1973

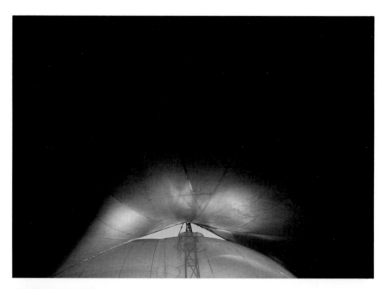

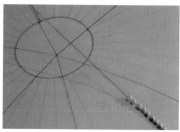

Symbiosis & Symbicle, imploded dome, 1982

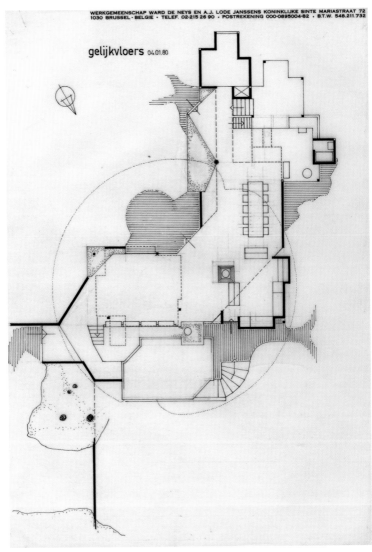

WERKGEMEENSCHAP WARD DE NEYS EN A.J. LODE JANSSENS KONINKLIJKE SINTE MARIASTRAAT 72
1030 BRUSSEL · BELGIE · TELEF. 02-215 26 90 · POSTREKENING 000-0895004-82 · B.T.W. 548.211.732

gelijkvloers 04.01.80

Symbiosis & Symbicle, the second home, 1982–2003

Symbiosis & Symbicle, the second home, before demolition, 2003

Symbiosis & Symbicle, the balloon home, 1981

Blueprint of test model tent structure Atelier Alpha, 1967

THE HANDKERCHIEF PRINCIPLE

Guy Mouton

It must have been roughly a quarter century ago that I received—as a structural engineer—an inquiry for my availability and interest in teaching a course on structural mechanics at the Sint-Lucas School of Architecture. I accepted the invitation and traveled to Brussels, where I had a meeting with the director and architect A.J. Lode Janssens. What followed was an exploration—a probing and gauging. We discussed the fundamental challenge of offering an abstract theoretical class like structural mechanics as part of an architecture curriculum.

Janssens strongly believed in giving insight into structural mechanics through physical demonstrations of structural distortions rather than via calculations. To underline the importance of insight acquired from empirical research, he asked me how it was possible that a handkerchief could not be pulled taut by pulling on its four corners. It was a problem he discovered in his investigations into tent structures. No matter how hard you pull, the central part of the textile remains slack. To my own frustration, I could not provide a clear answer.

Shortly afterward, I was thinking about the handkerchief problem and was able to supply an answer. I sent an unsolicited fax with a small handwritten exposé; I cannot recall if he ever replied.

A few basic laws of dynamics can explain how to put tension on parallel and perpendicular threads of fabric. The narrative of the fax was, and remains, for me a very graphic example of how one can introduce insights about structural mechanics into an architectural education. Lode was right!

Without formulas or calculations, the sketch showed how the tension of fabric works and offered insight into it (hopefully). Images can be used in a similar manner to explain other things, without having to develop analytic proofs. Students of architecture, after all, have different interests and possibly different ways of thinking than structural engineers. They are more concerned with how things work than why things work. Besides, there is no need for them to entirely understand certain analyses. Engineers are trained for this reason, and they end up doing that work for architects. In practice, it is a playful collaboration between architects, who create lasting architectural concepts, and engineers, who offer a structural basis to provide the architectural inventions with a dependable spine. That's the way it should be. In order to create interesting architectural concepts, architects need only understand the language of engineers—and engineers must be open to architectural creativity. When the architect—across the diverse fields to which architecture provides answers—can build a productive synthesis, and the knowledgeable engineer can give structural input, there's a good chance that a successful whole can emerge.

Philosopher Willem Koerse splits architectural design into first and second orders. It is obvious that the first order, which includes the structural design concept, needs to be well thought out if a long and sustainable life cycle is envisioned. The second order needs to be sufficiently interesting and offer the possibility for functions to change during the life cycle of a structure. This is crucial in determining the circularity of the building, for it is in the second order that functional changes take place. Thus, any necessary interventions in the first order need to be well designed to ensure that the circularity of that second order is not impaired. The preservation of that first order, or the total demolition of the building, will depend on different factors. Evident factors are the cultural and aesthetic context of the building and the place, while the polyvalent character of the first order and its structure can contribute to new possibilities. Therefore, structural elements need to be chosen carefully. The structural design concept needs to be intelligent, logical, supportive, and appropriate to the architectural idea. The task of the structural engineer, from this perspective, is as important as the architect's.

Returning to the point of how structural engineers can clarify things for architecture students, and how we can inspire their interest in the structural and constructional aspects of architecture: It is indeed not easy to explain how structures actually work. Formulas often do not provide the desired insight. Demonstrating how structures deform, also internally, does do that; or, at least, it provides a better understanding, even if it is not quantitative.

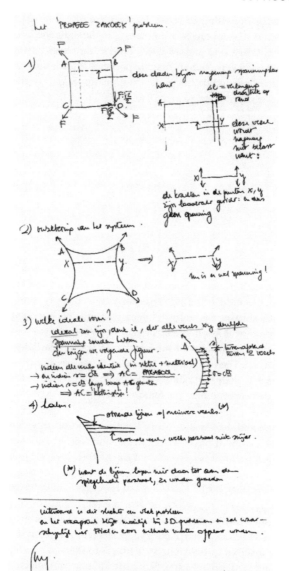

Fax from Guy Mouton to A. J. Lode Janssens on handkerchief logic, 1994

Using visual storytelling to show, for example, the internal forces of a cross-section of a beam can be a simple way to illustrate the internal forces of the beam. When one presses down on the middle of a thin (wooden) beam, it will bend. It is obvious that the particles at the bottom of the beam are being stretched, while the particles in the upper part of the beam are being compressed. But how can we show this?

The upper sketches show a beam resting on two support points and a force or weight in the middle. The beam has been divided into a number of slices. By internally shifting the support forces, two opposite but equal, horizontally balanced forces are created. The upper one compresses the upper particles, like in a column, and the other pulls at the lower particles, stretching out the material. The horizontally balanced forces are smaller in the slices that approach the support points of the beam, and therefore they are subject to less deformation than the middle slices.

How tension and deformation work together is beautifully demonstrated by the poetic work of the architect, artist, and teacher Paul Gees. Via his work, many structural principles can be explained and real insight can be offered. *In the right upper corner* (2004) creates a context for an engaged discussion. The principles he used to make the deformation visible—exploring which parts deform, which deform the most, and which parts don't deform at all—can be clearly explained. Sometimes, the artist deviates from the lower cross-sections to make his art pieces even more poetic. An artistically inspired quest! Here, structure is in dialogue with poetry and art—and also with architecture. Structure supports architecture, both literally and figuratively.

Post Scriptum

While jotting down these musings, I became acquainted, for the first time, with the plans of A.J. Lode Janssens' Balloon project. In all our years of working together, I never had the chance to see this project and he never told me about it either. I was completely surprised by it. What a beautiful and daring experiment! A fourteen-meter-wide, transparent balloon is dented into the ground plan and, under slightly elevated atmospheric pressure, is flanked by two protective tent structures—plus, a mast that pierces through—a challenge that Janssens did not shy away from and gave a surprisingly beautiful shape to. Both parts, dome and tents, are nicely taut, without any slackened parts. In short, the result of good and intense study work. The archive photos also reveal beautiful detailing: the dome lights up at night like a pearl in an open shell. Over the years, I have become convinced that in addition to a well-chosen structural design concept, the quality of the details is ultimately of the greatest importance. The edges of the tent structures are curved and not rectilinear as indicated by the clean handkerchief theory. Of course, A.J. Lode Janssens was aware of this... He put me to the test a quarter century ago, and he was just looking for a beautiful explanation.

Paul Gees, *In the right upper corner*, ashwood and stone, 2004

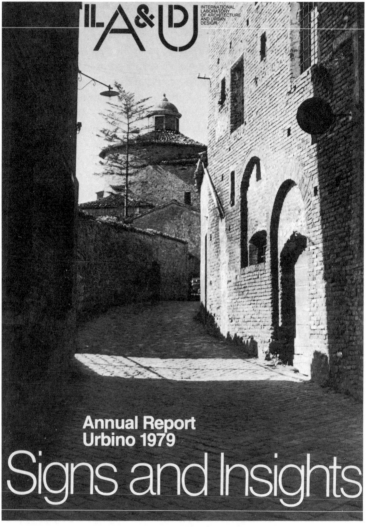

cover of the ILAUD yearbook, 1979

EDUCATION BETWEEN THOUGHT AND ACTION

Elke Couchez

On April 10, 1979, in a dilapidated building on Rogierstraat in Brussels, A.J. Lode Janssens and his colleague Evert Lagrou, who taught sociology at the Sint-Lucas School of Architecture and had gained experience in spatial and regional planning as an academic, opened their practice-based research office: the Sint-Lucas Werkgemeenschap, or the Sint-Lucas Working Community (SLuW).[1] The small-scale office offered an elective to four or five top-level fourth-year architecture students.[2] As an alternative to the desk crit- and drawing-based design studios at Sint-Lucas, SLuW guided students throughout a year-long "educational design office" experience, ending with an eight-week intensive Summer school in Italy, organized by the International Laboratory for Architecture and Urban Design (ILAUD). SLuW's ethos aimed at promoting community participation in decision-making processes and employing extensive research-based approaches in order to support local groups and residents. From 1979 to 1988, professors and students engaged in participative projects in complex areas in the Brussels agglomeration.

SLuW functioned as a hinge that joined institutionalized education, community service, and theoretical exchange on an international level. It was emblematic of Janssens' ambition to overthrow the binaries between working and thinking, action and thought, in his professional and pedagogical practices.

Triadic Constellations: Sint-Lucas, ILAUD, and SLuW

In the second half of the 1970s, the contours of architectural education at Sint-Lucas were fundamentally redrawn. Following a newly instated law on higher education, the school engaged in offering a full-time, "academic" five-year program in architecture.[3] As this process also required a well-considered institutional research policy and agenda, the then head of the architecture department Alfons Hoppenbrouwers asked Janssens to enroll in the newly established preparatory course "Licenses in Architecture Sciences" to prepare for a PhD at KU Leuven.[4] KU Leuven was involved in ILAUD from the very start. Instead of outlining his PhD project, Janssens became increasingly fascinated by ILAUD's educational model, one that resonated with his interest in participatory processes. He joined the KU Leuven delegation, led by Marcel Smets, to Urbino in 1979. One year later, Janssens formed a group with participants from Sint-Lucas Brussels and became from then on highly involved as an ILAUD staff member.

ILAUD was established in 1976, as an extension of Team X, by the architect and planner Giancarlo De Carlo. Each year, the ILAUD team invited leading research and educational institutions, and each delegated one or two staff members and five to six students to participate in a highly ambitious eight-week residential Summer course organized in a different Italian city. As one of many initiatives and networks centered on urbanism after the postwar reconstruction period, ILAUD offered a response to universalistic modernist planning models, haphazard urban renewal projects, and the imposition of a priori visions upon the city. Students and staff developed and tested tools for urban interventions and the reuse of existing buildings. Their design proposals were based on thorough understandings of the marks left by social, historical, and topographical transformations on physical space. By alternating between lectures, so-called readings of the territory, and design projects focused on specific areas in the city, the educational laboratory cultivated a pedagogy of reflection and action. In a letter to Peter Smithson, De Carlo wrote that he felt no need to establish yet another institutional school but wanted to create "a 'place' where different students from different countries meet, compare views, and outcomes of activities."[5] The goal of the Summer school, he continued, was to stimulate processes and not to design objects with "defined beginnings and ends."[6]

In preparation for the Summer school, all participants were expected to reflect on the year's central theme during a "permanent activities" program at each of the institutes. The topics of the formative ILAUD years were "Participation" and "Reuse."[7]

During the 1980 ILAUD Summer school, Janssens presented a SLuW project that had been commissioned by the Flemish Ministry of Culture. One of the ministry's agendas was to promote and represent Dutch-speaking communities within the French-oriented Brussels inner city. For this purpose, numerous buildings were acquired by the Flemish government and SLuW was asked to convert a former industrial site into a cultural meeting center, De Kriekelaar, for the Dutch-speaking community.[8] SLuW inventoried the building's physical conditions while performing an urban survey of the area "through an investigation of the existing regional and local planning programs, demographic situation, public transportation system, political structure of the city."[9] Following the inventory and mapping exercise, SLuW invited all stakeholders (the central government, cultural organizations, local communities) to define a potential program for the new center. However, SLuW abandoned the project in its final research phase, well before the project could be handed over to an implementing architectural office. According to Janssens, the project was targeted in a political smear campaign, leading to its suspension. In the complex politicized context of Brussels in the 1980s, De Kriekelaar added insult to injury. It painfully laid bare the sore patches of the so-called Brusselization, a term that was used internationally to refer to the profit-driven developments in urban cores, which demanded the demolition of historic buildings and neighborhoods.[10]

The De Kriekelaar project proved to be unsuccessful in the sense that it did not lead to the physical conversion of the built environment. However, the process enabled Janssens to outline his ambitions for SLuW. In the years to come, SLuW would work on commissions in close consultation with

A. J. Lode Janssens (right) and Evert Lagrou (left) at the presentation of the Brussels Metropolitan Plan, 1987

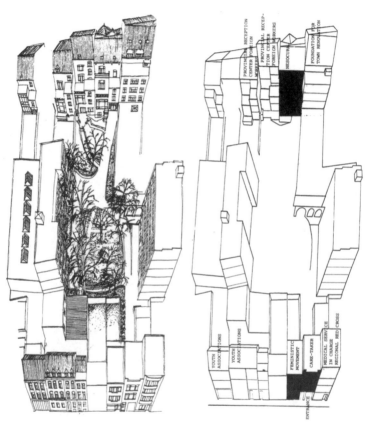

De Kriekelaar diagrams, Sint-Lucas Werkgemeenschap, 1985

officials and secretaries of state. The SLuW office inventoried the cultural infrastructure and social housing stock in Brussels (in 1980 and 1985) and drafted a metropolitan plan for Brussels (in 1987), among other analyses.

Experiential Models of Education

In addition to his presentation of SLuW's work in Brussels, Janssens presented the Balloon at the 1980 Summer school. He concluded his lecture with a provocative statement: "There is no more serious and intense form of thinking and working than playing."[11] When he used the word "play," he pointed to a deep-rooted divide in the sciences. As the philosopher Thomas Kuhn wrote in the early 1960s, scientists disagreed on the status of experimentation in scientific processes. In the classical tradition, the outcome of an experiment was presented in the form of law-like, universal generalizations. This model was questioned by modern science. The Baconian method stressed the exploratory—playful even—character of experimentation and rooted it in experience. "Experimentation" and "experience" are, after all, connected via the Latin root *experiri*, meaning "to try" or "to put to the test." In the Baconian view, experiments were carried out "with an eye for the local, contingent conditions that give rise to observed phenomena."[12]

This understanding of experimentation as experience was at the forefront of debate in the second half of the twentieth century in art and architecture education. Yet, as Eva Díaz notes, it was a porous category: "Experimentation can encompass practices that are incongruous, even fundamentally irreconcilable, and it's very porosity has often elided competing visions about spontaneity and rationality, improvisation and discipline, order and chaos, or the relationship of art and life that charged midcentury debates about it."[13] In this approach, the outcomes of trials could neither be forecasted or be generalized for broader applications. Since his overall design process allowed and playfully invoked the unknown and the unforeseen, A.J. Lode Janssens can be considered an heir of such Baconian tradition. In his Balloon research, the notions of experiment and experience became interchangeable. And it was precisely this intimate convolution that equally grounded his educational practice.

For Janssens, experimentation was a remedy against what he called a "catastrophic rift between thought and action" in architecture schools, which had led to siloed specialization or overly theoretical approaches.[14]

In his 1980 ILAUD lecture, Janssens pitted the playful combination of thinking and designing against the climate of "intellectualism" and "artistic elitism" at architecture schools and within academia. The question of how to challenge normative thinking was ubiquitous in the 1960s and 1970s, and led to pedagogical experimentation in and beyond architecture schools.

The traditional architecture studio course and its focus on design, rather than on building or experience, increasingly came to be perceived as an inadequate vehicle for preparing students for professional practice. This criticism was not new. Walter Gropius's holistic educational model at the Bauhaus already reestablished a critical relationship between the designer and material construction.[15] But it was only in the 1960s that design-build pedagogies, which engaged students in the design and construction of projects on site, gained new ground at universities. These programs not only advanced technical know-how and material knowledge, but also strengthened the ties with civil rights and environmentalist movements. The Yale Building Project was conceived by Charles W. Moore in 1967 and is a well-known example of a compulsory first-year graduate course that focused on developing low-cost housing and community development through direct engagement.[16] Also in the United States, the Institute of Architecture and Urban Studies (active from 1967 to 1984) combined research, education, and community development in an attempt to question traditional and academic models of architecture education outside the confines of a university setting.[17] In Europe, participative processes were instigated by influential architects such as De Carlo, Lucien Kroll, Ralph Erskine, Vernon Gracie, and Nicholas Habraken. SLuW shared with these programs the ambition to bring together research, education, and community service, but transferred each project to Signa, an architecture office focused on technical execution.

Design-build programs continue to influence curricula today: in Belgium, for instance, the Academic Design Offices established in the early 2000s at the Sint-Lucas School of Architecture (today the Faculty of Architecture, KU Leuven), the Stadsacademie at Universiteit Ghent, the Cosmopolis Centre for Urban Research at the Vrije Universiteit Brussel, and Live Projects at Universiteit Hasselt aspire to tackle societal challenges by connecting education and research to the professional field. Though the ambitions of these programs are increasingly met with pressures from the profession, they are instrumental in actively reimagining students' professional agency.

Linguistic Stalemate

Janssens' pedagogical experiments at Sint-Lucas were short-lived yet irrefutably impactful, not in the least through SLuW's insistence on establishing concrete discussions on the rationalization of architecture education through a stronger interlacing between spatial design and research. The educational model Janssens had in mind matched with the ideas De Carlo developed in ILAUD seminars. Both Janssens and De Carlo used the notion of "tentative design" to target the rift between thought and action.[18] For both educators, experimentation needed to be based on experience and action. Design was intrinsically bound to thinking and conceptualization, but a design solution did not linearly follow from the research problem.

In contemporary design education, the tangle between architectural design and research is still unresolved and very present. The eager use of notions such as "research by design," "design-oriented research," "design research," and "design thinking"—employed to outline the specific profile of the "thinking designer" in the last two decades—at times lapses into an inward-looking language play. By situating design against academic forms of knowledge production, these buzzwords risk consolidating the rift between thought and action, rather than overcome it. Janssens neither started nor solved this linguistic stalemate. But his educational project lays bare some of the biggest challenges of today's architecture education, in which the production of research has become highly marketable and monetized. A blind focus on research—and design as research—makes it easily co-optable by neoliberal market forces (education being part and parcel of that). "Research is the holy grail of contemporary architecture education," architecture historian Joan Ockman noted, and the "'laboratories' in which it is carried out—by white-coated architectural technicians, figuratively speaking—are its shrines."[19] In that light, Janssens' independent and philosophically inspired educational project can be read as a plea for the continuous questioning of the role of experimentation and experience in pedagogical processes and the need for an educational space that cherishes student-centered learning processes over consumable and marketable outcomes.

1   Janssens taught at Sint-Lucas from 1968 to 1990 and was the head of the architecture department from 1991 to 2003.

2   The team also consisted of research personnel and interns, one administrative clerk, and one technical draughtsperson.

3   For a detailed history, see Sofie De Caigny et al., eds., *Bronnengids architectuuronderwijs Vlaanderen* (Antwerp: Vlaams Architectuur-instituut, 2012).

4   The program prepared non-university-trained architects to develop a PhD trajectory. KU Leuven offered architecture education within the faculty of engineering. While Leuven, Gent University, and Vrije Universiteit Brussel were the only Belgian institutes that offered architecture education at a university level at that time.

5   Letter from Giancarlo de Carlo to Peter Smithson, December 12, 1977. ILAUD Archives, Biblioteca civica d'arte Luigi Poletti di Modena.

6   Ibid.

7   SLuW substantially contributed to the development of ILAUD topics, including "Multiplicity of Language," "Tentative Design," and "The Contemporary Town." In 1979, Janssens was also involved in the organization of the "Leuven Seminar on Participatory Design," a conference organized as part of ILAUD's permanent activities. The notes and summaries of the conference talks are collected in Marcel Smets, Jan Schreurs, and A.J. Lode Janssens, *Leuven Seminar on Participatory Design* (Leuven: Acco-Press, 1981).

8   This is described in closer detail in Patrick Blockx et al., "Hoger Sint-Lucas-instituut Brussels," in *International Laboratory of Architecture and Design: Annual Report, Urbino 1980* (Urbino: International Laboratory of Architecture and Design, 1980), 10–13.

9   Ibid., 12.

10 See Isabelle Doucet, *The Practice Turn in Architecture: Brussels after 1968* (Farnham: Ashgate Publishing, 2015), 12.

11 A.J. Lode Janssens, "Experimenting as a Form of Therapy," in *International Laboratory of Architecture and Design: Annual Report, Urbino 1980*, 58.

12 *New Dictionary of the History of Ideas*, ed. Maryanne Cline Horowitz (New York: Charles Scribner's Sons, 2005), s.v. "experimentation," 765.

13 Eva Díaz, *The Experimenters: Chance and Design at Black Mountain College* (Chicago: University of Chicago Press, 2015), 149.

14 Janssens, "Experimenting as a Form of Therapy," 58.

15 See Vincent Canizaro, "Design-Build in Architectural Education: Motivations, Practices, Challenges, Successes and Failures," *International Journal of Architectural Research* 6, no. 3 (2010): 20–36.

16 See Herbert S. Newman, "First Year Building Project: Learning Experience and Community Service," *Journal of Architectural Education* 34, no. 2 (1980): 26–28.

17 See Marianna Charitonidou, "From Harlem to New Haven: The Emergence of the Advocacy Planning Movement in the Late 1960s," in *Architecture and Democracy 1965–1989: Urban Renewal, Populism and the Welfare State*, ed. Dirk van den Heuvel et al. (Rotterdam: Het Nieuwe Instituut, 2019), 43.

18 For a deeper investigation on the notion of tentative design, see Elke Couchez, "Reading by Drawing — ILAUD 1977: A Tentative Tool for Urban Regeneration," *OASE* 107 (2020): 39–48.

19 Joan Ockman, "Slashed," e-flux architecture, October 2017, https://www.e-flux.com/architecture/history-theory/159236/slashed/.

LIVING AND BUILDING WITH AIR

Pieter Uyttenhove

I can't recall where exactly A.J. Lode Janssens' Balloon was erected, but I definitely did not hallucinate it. A few months ago, I accidentally found some slides from my visit there. It was the only time I saw the structure in person, as I never returned after my first time. I would sporadically happen upon it in architecture publications and I always wondered why it received so little attention in the architecture world. My confrontation with the structure was a revelation, and the impact that it had on me is hard to estimate. The Balloon embodied and concretized a lot of my architectural fantasies. However, I do not have any documentation that supports what I remember. There are only memories and interpretations of those memories. It can be argued that my slides hold more meaning than the published images do; they are biographical traces.

The group of five students with whom I visited the Balloon, in the spring of 1978, consisted of architecture engineering students. Three belonged to the so-called technicians of our year and were primarily interested in the rational and technical aspects of architecture. Then there was a good friend of mine, whose eye I greatly appreciated—he looked beyond the built, interested more in construction and materials; he seemed to empathize with the poetic dynamic of how the materials "worked." Incidentally, he would find great success after college as an artist in Brussels. He constructed sophisticated sculptures out of glass, steel, and concrete that were put under pressure or tension over many hours until, with agonizing slowness, they finally gave out. The groaning and moaning of the materials as they were tortured was magnified for the public by microphones mounted on the works. The fifth student was me. I wanted to experience something other than the column-and-beam structures and prefab elements we were exhaustingly emphasized in school. The diverse composition of the group summarized the different imaginaries triggered by the Balloon: technological performance, poetic materiality, construction principles, forms of alternative living, critical architecture, etc.

We enlisted in this field trip as part of Geert Bekaert's architecture history course. Our assignment was to write a group paper on an existing building. Bekaert had shortlisted possible buildings—the Balloon clearly

Symbicle docking sluice (never used), 1976

stood out. Why this Marxist architecture historian and theorist had included this building on his list of recent and historical buildings remained a mystery to us. According to our humble opinions, the reason must have had something to do with either the contemporality of the Balloon itself, its experimental nature, or its historical eccentricity. In any case, we considered it our task to approach this architecture very critically.

I was not well prepared at the time to deliver a solid architectural critique, although I did not lack motivation. As a leading Belgian architecture critic, Bekaert had introduced us to sociocritical analysis—a welcome relief and much closer to our youthful concerns than the sterile (although not always uninteresting) stylistic histories of churches and palaces that our other professors had taught. Bekaert had already given us a basic overview to the sociocritical by introducing a variety of authors, including Marc-Antoine Laugier, Jacques-François Blondel, Aldo Rossi, Eugène Viollet-le-Duc, Martin Heidegger, and Manfredo Tafuri, among others. He had also made us purchase Charles Jencks's *Modern Movements in Architecture* from 1973, which I immediately started reading. This book imagined the modern movement as pluralistic in its ideological underpinnings. Bekaert embraced the mental shift promoted in the book, but he also questioned the postmodern air surrounding it—something that was intentionally cultivated by Jencks. This crossed a critical red line of architectural ethics for thinkers like Bekaert and the entire architecture department. Architecture was more than a rhetorical discourse, and history was not purely a genealogy of ideas but a set of touchstones to understand our world. These ideas provided us with some intellectual ammunition to write a paper about the Balloon.

Other aspects of building practices—related to self-built housing, vernacular and bottom-up forms of organization, and alternative societies—were hardly covered in our architectural education. A few months before purchasing Jencks's book, I had ordered Lloyd Kahn and Bob Easton's book *Shelter*, published in the wake of *Domebook 1* and *2*. Just about everything included in *Shelter*—treehouses; huts and tents; subterranean spaces and caves; nomadic lifestyles; materials like wood, bamboo, rope, canvas, etc.—opened a new world of forms and techniques that professional architecture sought to condemn to craftmanship and self-building. It was obvious that a distinct culture of building and dwelling was well understood by the faraway Californian counterculture, operating as a laboratory that appreciated and applied the logic and techniques of old traditions and experimented with communal living as a way of opposing individualistic, suburban consumer society. This new culture was founded on ecological and sustainable principles, but also playful and creative approaches to dwelling and living environments.

The honorable vision of *Shelter* stood in stark contrast to the utopian and often ironic rhetoric of groups like Archizoom, Archigram, and Super-studio. Although these groups had passed their prime by several years, their conceptual power still enchanted many architecture students. Their paper architecture was often colossal in scale, composed of unspecified abstract materials that required highly specialized technical knowledge, and supported by mechanisms and machines to enable the functioning of this architecture. A year earlier, I had had a taste of these contradictions during a visit to Munich. I had gone to see the tent structures Frei Otto designed for the 1972 Olympics. The scale was so immense that the playful concept of canvas and cables had become static and motionless in its gigantic dimensions. All possible traces of handcraft and natural

Olympic Games Tent, Frei Otto, Munich, 1972

suppleness were stiffened by industrially produced, large-scale nodes, nuts, bolts, and cables with decimeter diameters. It illustrated the gap between imagination and actual experience, between metaphor and reality. Influenced by these conceptual utopians, and having considered all its dimensions, we unconsciously imagined Janssens' Balloon as a shining and transparent high-tech dome in the middle of an inhospitable desert.

Toward the end of the drive to the Balloon, the road passes rural parcels of Belgian villas and neo-farmsteads, until we arrive at the correct address where we see little, almost nothing. A dirt driveway, paved with a few commercial tiles, winds its way into some trees further up. Among the trees, about fifty meters away, we discern a large tent roof. It must be here! At the beginning of the driveway, a big round air vent is sticking out of the ground (it turned out to be a mailbox). A.J. Lode Janssens, padded by a parka and with a slender posture with wild hair and a beard, welcomes us with a large smile. His wife and children are also present, as well as an immense Great Dane that overtakes us. We receive an elaborate tour and have a long conversation. Every possible question we have is answered at length, with joyful openness. Janssens is a good communicator and an excellent pedagogue.

From the first moment we encounter it, the dwelling surprises, overwhelms. Here, many clichés of the suburban home fall apart, not because of ideology but because of the daily practice and logic of the building. Closing the front door to prevent a draft from blowing in, for example, is something we are used to; but having to close the sluice in order to keep in the overpressure inside, as is done here, turns that logic on its head. In the Balloon, inside and outside have a special relationship to one another. The dome creates a central space in the middle of a little forest, whose trees rises up all around and sway in the wind. You can hear the woods as if you are standing in it. The Balloon has been entrenched several meters into the ground, and the displaced earth serves as hilly windbreaks around it. The indoor climate is undeniably unusual and far from stable. The sun quickly warms up the space inside, but every passing cloud also instantly has a cooling effect. The inhabitants live on the whims of nature. Partially covering the Balloon, the outer canvas is meant to mitigate the influence of the weather. Tarps, surrounding walls, and uneven landscape features create a place that is protected. The Balloon is alive as it wobbles in the wind; the glued seams, however, can only take a certain amount of stress before tearing. Thin tensile cables across the meridians of the skin stabilize it. The large vertical truss column, located in the indoor space, passes through a protrusion at its top to exit the structure. Attached to this tower, which can pivot to absorb minimal movements, are the outer canvasses.

In the center of the communal living space—where the kitchen, library, and spaces for sitting, working, and eating are located—is an orange floating volume (mounted on a support structure) that is strongly reminiscent of Archigram's *Living Pod* from 1967. It contains the parent's sleeping quarters. Additional rooms for the children and other smaller spaces are built in hard materials like Plexiglas and annexes built of metal profiles are attached to main space. Outside, large pipes disappear into the ground— they are responsible for the air supply, connected to pumps that keep the air volume in the Balloon under pressure. Adjacent to these, a large vertical pipe serves as a chimney for the combustion gasses of the heating system.

The technology of the Balloon is rudimentary, appropriate to human scale, and improvised, in the sense that the project is essentially a form of pioneering. There was no tangible example to follow and learn from. Moreover, the technology is not trying to make a statement. Instead, it simply supports a project that is first and foremost an experiment in building, dwelling, and co-living. Dwelling and co-living as an experiment, in this case, are limited to their own circle of family and friends. It was never Janssens' intension to initiate a movement for testing co-living typologies, especially not in this suburban environment that inherently stimulates individualism.

The Balloon is hardly related to what is happening in the urban centers of Brussels, Antwerp, Gent, Amsterdam, or London. There, experiments and collective actions are taking place against the demolition of the city, against the eviction and displacement of poor residents, and against the vacancy of habitable buildings.

Janssens does not seek to demonstrate autocracy, or an off-grid lifestyle, in the banal suburban surroundings of the Balloon. In his decision to live in such a structure, he seeks to experience how dwelling and building converge, as well as how time is actually the experience of being present in a specific place. The Balloon is the experimental laboratory for these Heideggerian statements. In its design, Janssens chose a place and built a home that would feel like the place itself. The dwelling changes the place but is also shaped by it.

The Balloon's air vents, 1976

Daily life requires constant building. The humidity of the forest and the moss of the tree branches deposit themselves on the Balloon and its tarpaulins. When the plastic becomes dirty and opaque, Janssens wipes clean several surfaces, which thus resemble windows. The quiet but constant movement of the Balloon, and the sliding and rubbing of the tensile cables across the plastic, risk damaging or tearing the balloon skin. For this reason, orbs have been mounted along the cables. The nodes where the canvas and cables are attached consist of metal parts that can be purchased in a standard hardware store. Outside, underneath the tarpaulins, a space has been created for car parking and other storage. Inside the living room, a television antenna is attached to the central tower. Over time, leaks in the annexed window coves, made out of glued Plexiglas, are repaired with asphalt tape. Dwelling requires daily creativity and problem solving.

Dwelling is building and building is dwelling. Janssens is acutely aware of this. He builds with air. It is the structural framework for his Balloon—like in Ant Farm's inflatables in California. The materials and techniques used are fragile, with a short lifespan of a dozen years or so. His experiment is a critique of consumer society that has taken over architecture—from the concept of the architect to the building materials of the contractor and wholesaler, from the technological conditioning of indoor and outdoor spaces to the gross denial of place. A.J. Lode Janssens' Balloon is a criticism of contemporary dwelling, a criticism of the fact that constructive thinking and acting, with regard to one's own destiny and life, has all too much been put in the hands of third parties.

The guided garden, 1976

Ant Farm, *50×50' Pillow*, temporary installation, Freestone, California, 1970

A.J. LODE JANSSENS

1979

Herman Selleslags

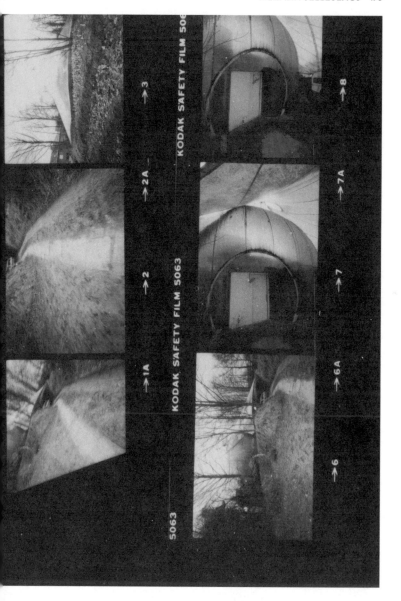

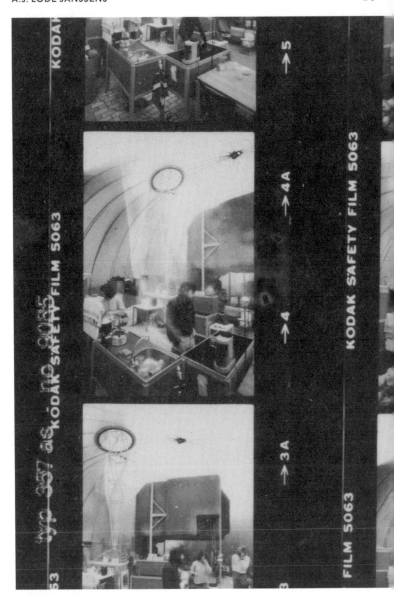

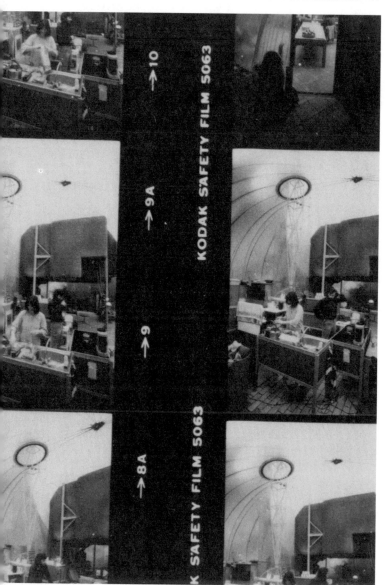

KODAK S'AFETY FILM 5063

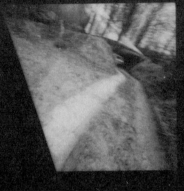

→1A

5063 KODAK S'AFETY FIL

→6 →6A

KODAK SAFETY FILM 5063

→2A   →3   →3A

KODAK SAFETY FILM 5063

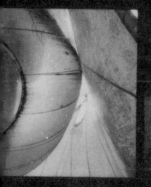

→7A   →8   →8A

A.J. Lode Janssens, with the Atelier Alpha blueprint, 2021

A.J. LODE JANSSENS
Born 1941, Humbeek (B)
Prof. Architect-Urbanist, 1964–2003

Architectural Practice
Communal architectural practice
Atelier Alpha with Willy Van Der
Meeren, 1964–68
Communal architectural practice
Werkgemeenschap '70 with
Ward De Neys, Jef Cochez,
1970–78
Individual architectural practice,
1964–92

Built Projects
1964 House Robberechts, Kapelle-
op-den-Bos
House De Mey, Zaventem
1965 House Pulinx, Koningslo
House Roelants, Koningslo
House Van der Veken,
Humbeek
1966 Experimental Atelier Alpha
building, Sterrebeek, with
Willy Van Der Meeren
1967 House Verhelpen, Grimbergen
House Dupay, Humbeek
HBK office competition,
with Willy Van Der Meeren
(laureate)
1968 House De Buyser, Humbeek
House Engels, Humbeek
House Buggenhout,
Nieuwenrode
1969 House Thielemans, Strombeek
House Verdickt, Humbeek
House Van Campenhout,
Humbeek
Weekend House De Cooman,
Meldert
House Van Hemelrijck,
Humbeek
House De Hertogh, Wolvertem
Sportsfields & Sportcentre,
Humbeek
Experimental living project
Symbiose & Symbicle, Hum-
beek, 1969–82
1970 House De Hertog, Elewijt
House De Bruyne, Grimbergen
House De Roover, Grimbergen
Printshop ADB Andries,
Humbeek
National Idea Competition
Centre Civique, Limal, with
Jef Cochez (laureate)
Urban plan Town Centre,
Limal, with Ward De Neys

Chapel and Altar Parish
Church, Humbeek
1971 Shop House De Lange,
Strombeek
Kindergarten and Primary
School, Limal, with
Ward De Neys
Milling & Silo Company
Steenacker extension,
Meise
1972 Weekend house De Lange,
Kester
House Delefortrie, Kapelle-
op-den-Bos
House Keymolen, Leefdaal
House Moens, Beigem
Clarkson Offices, refurbish-
ment, Brussels
1973 House Janssens, Humbeek
House Dierickx, Humbeek
House Dieleman, Grimbergen
House Van Ackeleyen,
Grimbergen
1974 House Vanderminnen,
Humbeek
House Vandenbranden,
Humbeek
Alternative Interior, Interieur
Biënale, Kortrijk
Theaterlab Workshop,
Brussels
1975 House Van de Steen,
Sint-Denijs Westrem
Garden and play garden,
Kakelbont School, Brussels
Flower shop Lalu, Brussels
1976 Refurbishment House Mels,
Erps-Kwerps
Fire safety study
College Refectory, Zwijnaarde
1977 House De Rouck, Sinaai
Refurbishment House
Verlende, Merchtem
Masterplan Don Bosco
School, St.-Denijs-Westrem
1978 House Van Haegendoren,
Sint-Joris Weert
1979 Solar House De Decker,
Sint-Genesius-Rode
Masterplan Don Bosco
School, Hoboken
1980 Solar House De Groote,
Breendonk
Masterplan Don Bosco
School, Helchteren
Workshops and sports com-
plex Don Bosco, Hoboken
1984 Patio House Timmermans,
Humbeek

Masterplan Don Bosco
School, Kortrijk
1985 House De Sopper, Humbeek
1986 Brewery reconversion,
37 living units, Sint-Agatha-
Berchem, with Sint-Lukas
Werkgemeenschap
Headquarters and auditoria
Katholieke Industriële
Hogeschool, Antwerp
1990 House Vinken, Beigem
1991 Insurance Offices Moens,
Humbeek
1992 Pre-design Meurop Education
Complex
Sint-Lucas School of Architec-
ture, Brussels

Education & Research
Sint-Lucas School of Architecture,
Brussels & Ghent
Professor Interior Architecture
Design Atelier, 1968–78
Professor Architecture Design,
1978–90
Founder of Stichting Sint-Lukas-
werkgemeenschap, with
Evert Lagrou, 1979
Board Member ILAUD, 1980–90
Head of Department, Sint-Lucas
School of Architecture, Brussels
& Ghent, 1991–2003

Visiting Lecturer
Strassbourg (atelier Gaetano
Pesce), Lund & Stockholm (atelier
Bengt Edman), Oslo (atelier Sverre
Fehn), Grenoble (atelier Bruno
Quesanne)

A.J. LODE JANSSENS

Elke Couchez is a historian whose work explores the intersections between the intellectual history of architecture and urban design, visual studies, and pedagogy. In 2018 and 2019, she worked as a postdoctoral fellow on the project "Is Architecture Art?" at the University of Queensland's Centre for Architecture, Theory, Criticism and History. As a Research Foundation Flanders (FWO) Senior Postdoctoral Fellow at Hasselt University, she teaches art and architecture history and works on a research project entitled "Pedagogical Tools and Design Strategies for Urban Regeneration: International Laboratory for Architecture & Urban Design (1976–2015)."

Bart Decroos is an architect and academic researcher based in Antwerp. He is currently a PhD candidate at the University of Antwerp. He is a member of the editorial board of *OASE* and writes for various architecture magazines.

Filip Dujardin is an architecture photographer and visual artist. Alongside photographing existing buildings for architects, he creates digital photocollages of fictious architecture, which he also translates into sculptural installations. These "fictions" were shown for the first time at the Centre for Fine Arts/Bozar Brussels in 2007 and have since been exhibited around Europe and the United States. His work has been acquired by several museums and private collections, including the Metropolitan Museum of Art and MoMA in New York and San Francisco MoMA.

Marc Godts free architect, lives and works.

Nikolaus Hirsch is an architect, curator, and educator. He is the Artistic Director of CIVA in Brussels, and previously was the director of Städelschule and Portikus in Frankfurt. He has taught at the Architectural Association and Columbia University. His architectural work includes the Dresden Synagogue, Hinzert Document Center, Cybermohalla Hub Delhi, and *Do We Dream Under The Same Sky* at Art Basel and LUMA in Arles. His work has been exhibited at Manifesta 7, Chicago Architecture Biennale, and ZKM Karlsruhe. Hirsch curated *Folly* at the Gwangju Biennale, *Housing Question* at HKW Berlin, and the German Pavilion at the Venice Biennale in 2021. He is the author of the books *On Boundaries* (2007) and *Cybermohalla Hub*, (2012) editor of the Critical Spatial Practice series published by Sternberg Press, and founder of e-flux Architecture.

Guy Mouton is an architect and engineer. He taught at the architecture school at KU Leuven from 1994 to 2015. His structural design firm focuses on creating an optimal synergy between structure and architecture. His projects include the library in Ghent known as De Krook (Coussée Goris Huyghe architecten, in cooperation with RCR Arquitectes), the Antwerp Port Authority (Zaha Hadid Architects), and Beurshal and Congresgebouw in Bruges (META architectuurbureau, in cooperation with Eduardo Souto de Moura).

Herman Selleslags is a Belgian photographer who captures daily life in a no-nonsense manner. His reporting and documentary work, mainly shot in black and white, range from iconic portraits over rock and sports photography to (inter)national events. Since 2015, Selleslags' archives are part of the Antwerp Photo Museum collection.

Peter Swinnen is a Brussels-based architect. After graduating from the Architectural Association in London and Sint-Lucas Brussels, and an apprenticeship at Luc Deleu & T.O.P. office, he founded 51N4E with Lieven De Boeck, which he spearheaded for fifteen years. Between 2010 and 2015, Swinnen served as the Flemish Government Architect, a public and independent political mandate that sought to empower architecture as a policy-whispering discipline. Since 2015 he has been co-principal and senior architect at CRIT. Swinnen has taught at the Architectural Association, KU Leuven, La Cambre, University of Luxembourg, and ETH Zurich. He has written and edited numerous books and texts including, *Double or Nothing* (2011), *Reasons for Walling a House* (2012), *René Heyvaert* (2019), *Luc Deleu & T.O.P. office: Future Plans 1970–2020* (2020), *Le Musée et Son Double* (2020), *Red Luxembourg* (2022), and *I Prefer Not To* (2022).

Pieter Uyttenhove is a professor of the history and theory of urbanism at Ghent University. He has published widely in international journals and is the author and editor of several books. His latest book (with Bart Keunen and Lieven Ameel) is *La puissance projective: Intrigue narrative et projet urbain* (2021). He was the Peter Paul Rubens Chair for Flemish Studies at the University of California, Berkeley, in 2019.

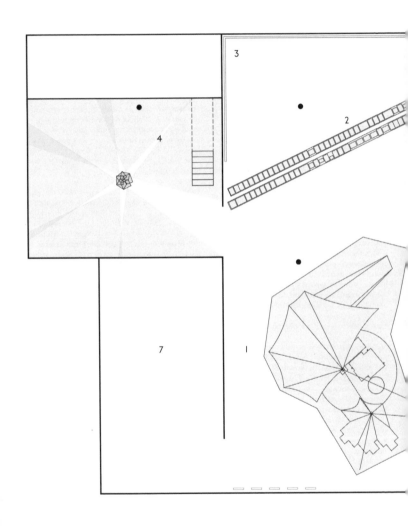

CRIT. architects, exhibition floorplan for "A.J. Lode Janssens: A Balloon Home,"
CIVA, Brussels, December 10, 2021–March 27, 2022

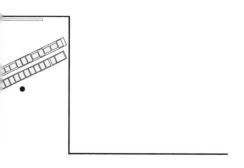

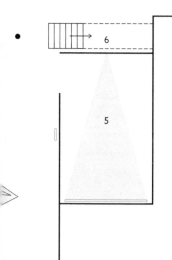

1   Balloon Home 1973–82
    (scale 1/4 model by CRIT.
    architects & DNA, 2021)
2   Private Archives 1969–82
    (courtesy of A.J. Lode
    Janssens)
3   Panorama 1979 (courtesy of
    CIVA archives)
4   Slide Archive 1969–82
    (courtesy of A.J. Lode
    Janssens), interpreted by
    Marc Godts (Slide Monster,
    2021)
5   Three movie short-cuts
    1971–77 (courtesy of VRT)
6   The After-Home 1982–2000
    (courtesy of A.J. Lode
    Janssens)
7   Education Room (courtesy
    of Masterstudio Interior
    Architecture Performatieve
    Ruimte en Nabijheid, KUL
    Faculty of Architecture,
    Campus Sint-Lucas, 2021)

PHOTOCREDITS

© A.J. Lode Janssens
p. 6, 10, 12–13, 17–18, 27, 48, 54,
56–57, 59, 62, 66, 68, 70, 72, 76,
81–95, 98–103, 110–27, 138–44, 148,
153–54
© Ant Farm, UC Berkeley Art
Museum and Pacific Film Archive
p. 168–69
© Comune di Modena
p. 150
© François Dallegret 1965
© SABAM Belgium 2021
p. 53
© Filip Dujardin
p. 33–47
© Luc Gees
cover, p. 8, 104–09
© Paul Gees
p. 149
© Guy Mouton
p. 147–48
© Jos Vandenbreeden © CIVA –
Sint-Lukasarchief
p. 30–31, 52, 61, 65, 128–37
© Pieter Uyttenhove
p. 96–97, 160, 162, 164–65, 167
© Herman Selleslags
p. 171–83
© Peter Swinnen/CRIT.
p. 184, 188–89

PUBLICATION

Editors
Peter Swinnen & Nikolaus Hirsch

Concept
Peter Swinnen/CRIT.

Design
Kim Beirnaert

Coordination
Tania Garduño Israde

Authors/Contributors
Elke Couchez
Bart Decroos
Filip Dujardin
Nikolaus Hirsch
A.J. Lode Janssens
Guy Mouton
Herman Selleslags
Peter Swinnen
Pieter Uyttenhove

Archive assistants
Danny Casseau
Luc Nagels

Translation
Atelier Orlando

Copy editing
Leah Whitman-Salkin
Anne Judong

Printing and binding
die Keure, Brugge

Published by
CIVA
Rue de l'Ermitage 55
1050 Brussels
www.civa.brussels

Spector Books
Harkortstraße 10
04107 Leipzig
www.spectorbooks.com

Distribution
Germany, Austria:
GVA, Gemeinsame Verlags-
auslieferung Göttingen GmbH
& Co. KG
www.gva-verlage.de
Switzerland:
AVA Verlagsauslieferung AG
www.ava.ch
France, Belgium:
Interart Paris, www.interart.fr

UK:
Central Books Ltd
www.centralbooks.com
USA, Canada, Central and South
America, Africa:
ARTBOOK | D.A.P.
www.artbook.com
Japan:
twelvebooks
www.twelve-books.com
South Korea:
The Book Society
www.thebooksociety.org
Australia, New Zealand:
Perimeter Distribution
www.perimeterdistribution.com

© 2022 Spector Books

© 2022 A.J. Lode Janssens, CRIT./Peter
Swinnen, authors and contributors.

First edition

Printed in the EU

ISBN 978-3-95905-602-1